WHY
LINCOLN
MATTERS

MARIO M. CUOMO

WHY LINCOLN MATTERS

Today More Than Ever

HAROLD HOLZER
historical consultant

HARCOURT, INC.
Orlando   Austin   New York   San Diego   Toronto   London

www.HarcourtBooks.com

Library of Congress Cataloging-in-Publication Data
Cuomo, Mario Matthew.
Why Lincoln matters: today more than ever/Mario M. Cuomo;
Harold Holzer, historical consultant.—1st ed.
p.   cm.
ISBN 0-15-100999-6
1. Lincoln, Abraham, 1809–1865—Political and social views.
2. Lincoln, Abraham, 1809–1865—Influence. 3. United States—
Politics and government—2001– 4. United States—Foreign relations—
2001– 5. United States—Economic conditions—2001–
6. United States—Social conditions—1980–
I. Holzer, Harold.   II. Title.
E457.2.C945   2004
973.7'092—dc22   2004001621

Text set in Centaur
Designed by Linda Lockowitz

Printed in the United States of America

First edition
A C E G I K J H F D B

CONTENTS

The struggle of today is not altogether for today;
it is for a vast future also.

—ABRAHAM LINCOLN
ANNUAL MESSAGE TO CONGRESS
DECEMBER 3, 1861

INTRODUCTION

FOR A LONG TIME we have been the most powerful nation in the world, with the mightiest military, the largest economy, and a unique history of providing opportunity for generations of searchers and strugglers. Millions of people in other parts of the world would give almost anything to live here; hundreds die every year trying to come to this country illegally. And precious few Americans are eager to leave.

As great as we have been, it is also apparent that we are not nearly as strong, rich, successful, and respected a nation as we could be if only we used our resources and opportunities better. We have fragmented ourselves into a three-tiered democracy with a small but growing number of extravagantly wealthy people, a majority of workers and retirees struggling not to slide back down the economic ladder, and a significant minority of Americans—as many as 35 million people, including 11 million children—mired in poverty. And, although we are the richest and most powerful nation in the world, we are also at a low point in our standing with other nations—including many in our own hemisphere.

In recent years we have seemed unable to decide exactly what we want to be as a nation. We have been tempted to see ourselves as fifty separate states or worse—280 million disassociated individuals struggling for survival or dominance in a dog-eat-dog world—instead of seeing ourselves as members of a fully integrated society, interconnected, interdependent, growing stronger together by sharing benefits and burdens.

Then on 9/11, without warning, like missiles from hell, two planes filled with innocent captives smashed into the twin towers of the World Trade Center, obliterating those majestic monuments to our nation's success. The explosions reduced the buildings to ugly black clouds of ash-bearing smoke and gargantuan piles of rubble that contained the remains of nearly three thousand human beings.

At first we were stunned, almost disbelieving. Then, as more and more of the grotesque details were revealed, the nation was wracked with anguish and rage. Two thoughts pressed themselves on us. The first was the frightening revelation that there are in this world people—perhaps *many* people—who hate us so much that they would eagerly give up their lives to take ours. And the second was the pathetically unanswerable question: "Why would any good God allow this to happen to innocent people?"

Before long these questions were put aside. The president directed the beginning of a war against terrorism, and the whole nation joined in supporting our attacks in Afghanistan against the Taliban, al-Qaeda, and Osama bin Laden, who boasted of leading the terrorists' "victory" over the "Great Satan."

Gradually, as the battle lagged in Afghanistan and bin Laden continued to elude our forces, uncertainty began to replace sureness in the minds of the nation's people. It grew into real doubt as the result of a series of decisions by President George W. Bush. He suddenly redirected our forces from Afghanistan to Iraq. Over the protests of some of our major allies he went to war against that nation, insisting that Saddam Hussein possessed weapons of mass destruction and was complicit with Osama bin Laden and al-Qaeda and that he was, therefore, a serious, imminent threat to the United States. We bombed Baghdad; killed thousands of Iraqis, most of them innocent; lost hundreds of our troops; and captured Saddam Hussein. But we never found any weapons of mass destruction or evidence of complicity with bin Laden.

Some people accused the president of having lied to the American people; however, it seems more plausible that he was misled by faulty intelligence and zealous aides. In either case he lost considerable credibility, causing his belated assertion that the rationale for the attack on Iraq was really an attempt to liberate the Iraqis from tyranny to appear to be nothing but a convenient afterthought.

Now we find ourselves stuck in Iraq with more than 100,000 of our troops on constant guard against guerrilla opponents who have killed or wounded more than 500 American soldiers since the fall of Baghdad.

It is not clear when the occupation will end or if it is possible for the Iraqis to govern themselves with some form of democracy. It is also not exactly clear what effect on terrorism our "victory" in Iraq has had and whether or not there is any comprehensive and effective plan for the continuing war against terrorism. Nor does the administration appear to know how to win back the valuable friendship of most of the world's major nations. It is not even apparent that it wants to.

All these unanswered questions about our foreign policy, together with a long list of serious domestic concerns, are at the heart of the political debate in the 2004 campaign for president. The issues have divided the American people almost exactly in half as they were in the 2000 election when a one-vote margin in the Supreme Court made George W. Bush president even though at least 500,000 more voters had chosen Vice President Al Gore at the polls.

At this writing it appears that our nation will probably come out of the current election no closer to agreement than it was then, especially since neither party so far has presented a compelling, comprehensive, achievable vision that sets out the basic principles we must live by to bring us closer to the more perfect Union described by our Founding Fathers.

Our president, upon whom—according to the test of incumbent presidents formulated by Ronald Reagan in 1980—rests the burden of proving we are better off today than we were four years ago, appears to be relying on a presumption of continuance instead of a comprehensive vision.

Given the much weaker economy, poor job creation, the growing disparity in wealth, high unemployment, and confused foreign policy, George W. Bush does not have much choice other than to seek a second term on a collection of specific vote-getting measures calculated to get him the support he will need to win in November—things like dubious schemes to welcome illegal aliens, promised trips to the Moon and Mars, $1.5 billion to teach people how to get married and stay married, a constitutional amendment to ban gay marriages, and still more tax cuts. He cannot plausibly run as President Reagan did by making his basic mission the shrinking of government, given the extravagance, flatulence, and imbalance in his own budgets. Nor can he recycle his "compassionate conservative" label in view of his demonstrated, distinct preference for the wealthy and self-sufficient over the millions of Americans in need of more and better health care, education, and retirement security.

The Democrats, on the other hand, spent most of their time so far bashing the president and bruising one another in the early primary season and have not yet delivered their own complete and persuasive alternate agenda.

So far in the campaign, therefore, the American people have been besieged with political attacks and discourse that seem largely contradictory, incomplete, and ineffectual as a platform around which Americans might coalesce. Republicans offer the menacing power of our armed forces, the willingness to use it preemptively; and the alleged fortification of our homeland defenses against terrorism from abroad as their foreign policy; and by way of domestic policy they favor constant supply-side tax cuts for the wealthy accompanied by cuts in benefits to those still struggling. That's hardly the kind of inspirational agenda that will unify a nation. Nor are we likely to be moved by the Democrats if all they offer is their own version of compassionate conservatism or a barrage of negative attacks on the Republicans with no overarching grand concept of their own.

That's what the nation needs—an overarching grand concept. We are preoccupied with the memory of 9/11 and the urgent necessity to stop the assassins from continuing a plague of terrorism that has existed for at least twenty years during several presidential administrations, but we shudder to think that the strongest legacy our generation will leave behind is our reputation for succeeding at killing and warmongering without making ourselves as safe as we once felt. We are left with no reassuring political orthodoxy, no uplifting cause, no inspiring rationale. We yearn for a vision worthy of the world's greatest nation.

With all his imperfections, that is what Abraham Lincoln brought us—and can help bring us again. It is no surprise that for generations, politicians have twisted themselves—and Lincoln—out of shape to make it appear that they are standing next to the sixteenth president. His achievements make him irresistible, and his eloquence makes him easy to quote. Articles and books have been written describing Lincoln as a liberal; others have been written claiming him as a conservative. But there is no political label elastic enough to fit around his magnificent complexity. No label does justice to his complicated combination of strengths and vulnerabilities, his genius and insufficiencies, his brilliant boldness and wise pronouncements.

Conservatives and liberals alike should always resist the impulse to make Lincoln over in their own image. Lincoln is too good and valuable to be used that way. But it would be even worse not to use him as he might be used. We should not be so awestruck by the towering figure that history and legend have made of him that we are reluctant to ask him to help us understand and deal with some of today's challenges.

Lincoln speaks to us today as he did more than 150 years ago because he spoke to the ages, to his own countrymen, to his brothers and sisters worldwide. He does it with eloquent simplicity as he did when he spoke in Trenton, New Jersey, on his way to his inauguration:

> Back in my childhood, the earliest days of my being able to read, I got hold of a small book . . . "Weems's Life of Washington." I remember all the accounts there given of the battlefields and struggles for the liberties of the country, and . . . the great hardships endured at that time, all fixed themselves on my memory. . . . I recollect thinking then, boy even though I was, that there must have been something more than common that those men struggled for. I am exceedingly anxious that that thing which they struggled for; that something even more than national independence; that something that held out a promise to all the people of the world to all time to come . . . shall be perpetuated in accordance with the original idea for which the struggle was made.[1]

Here was Lincoln "with a task before me greater than that which rested upon Washington," reminding us of the source of his strength and eventual greatness and expressing a compelling need to understand the meaning of things and to commit to a course that was directed by reason, supported by principle, sanctified by history, and designed to achieve the greatest good.[2] Lincoln was a man of ideas, large and soaring ones; and as he was cursed by the realization that they were achievable so he could not escape the obligation

1. February 21, 1861, Roy P. Basler et al., eds., *The Collected Works of Abraham Lincoln*, 9 vols. Hereinafter cited as *Collected Works*. (New Brunswick, NJ: Rutgers University Press, 1953–55), 4:235–36.
2. February 11, 1861, in ibid., 4:190.

of pursuing them with actions, despite the peril and the pain of doing so.

Even as a boy he grasped the single most important idea that would sustain him—and provoke him—for the rest of his days. The proposition that all men are created equal became the thread of purpose that tied the boy to the man and then to the legend. The achievable dream of equality and opportunity for all was the "original idea" for which the struggle was made: the idea that all men are endowed by the Creator with certain unalienable rights—life, liberty, and the pursuit of happiness.

To Lincoln this wasn't just a lovely, lofty dream or divine poetry to soothe the soul by wrapping it in high aspiration. It was the specific, achievable goal of flesh-and-blood humans who would have to find ways to provide education, food, employment, security from assault, and, most of all, equality of opportunity and the right to be treated with dignity for all people. He understood it could not be spoken or prayed into existence, rather it would have to be built by the work of our hearts and hands, consistently and patiently.

From the time Lincoln read Weems's "small book" until the day he was martyred, he thought, worried, planned, prayed, and labored to make the words of the Declaration of Independence a way of life. Equality and opportunity for all—truly for *all*.

Lincoln understood from the beginning that this was a promise that could only be fulfilled by degrees, step-by-step, sometimes painfully, until finally everyone in his own land and all over the globe reaped its benefits. Until this vision was achieved, the bold aspiration set forth in the Declaration would not be redeemed. For him this was the unifying principle of our democracy. Without it we had no nation worth fighting for. With it we had no limit to the good we might achieve here in our own land and in the great world beyond.

Lincoln believed that the new freedom included not only the right to live free from oppression but also the right— and the obligation—to try to achieve human betterment by helping one another through sharing. So he reached out for the "penniless beginner" and insisted every "poor man" should be given his chance. And he knew that it would not be enough to achieve this goal in his own land alone. It would have to be accomplished everywhere for there to be true fulfillment and peace in the world. He saw what others could not see: that it was the immensity of the fundamental ideas of freedom and self-determination that made his young nation such a radically new adventure in government and that if it succeeded here it would be a beacon to all the world's people still struggling to achieve dignity. But if it failed, it might extinguish the flame of liberty for untold millions around the world.

So he offered the poor more than freedom and the encouragement of his own good example—he offered them a government that would work aggressively to help them find the chance they might not have found alone. Lincoln did it by fighting for projects of "internal improvements" that others decried as excessive government. He gave help for education, agriculture, and the rural homemaker. And he helped obtain land for those who, without government, would have had no hope for it. At the time, most politicians were saying that government should do no more than protect its people from foreign enemies and insurrection and should spend the rest of its time dispassionately observing the way its people played out the cards that fate had dealt them. He scorned that view; he called it a "do nothing" abdication of governmental responsibility. "The legitimate object of government," he said, "is to do for a community of people, whatever they need to have done, but can not do, *at all*, or can not, so *well* do, for themselves—in their separate, and individual capacities."[3]

At the heart of his struggle and his yearning was always the passion to make room for the outsider and the insistence upon a commitment to respect the idea of equality by fighting for inclusion. Diversity, he said, was not a matter of discord, but a true bond of union. He looked beyond the superficial differences that God or history had imposed on us to see the essential truths that unite us. He sympathized vigorously with the cause of democracy in other lands—in Hungary and Mexico and Greece.[4] He understood that a respect for individual dignity and the equality of all people was the essential foundation not just for his American family but for the whole human race. Were he alive today, Lincoln would express no shock at learning that there were millions of people around the world—in the Middle East, in Africa, and in other places—whose poverty, lack of freedom, and lack of self-esteem make them dangerous enemies to those more fortunate people who might be perceived as oppressing them, aiding their oppressors, or denying them the help they need to earn their own share of comfort and security.

---

3. ca. July 1, 1854, in *Collected Works*, 2:220. Lincoln wrote a slightly different version of this sentiment at the same time.

4. For Lincoln and Hungary, see, for example, resolutions in support of Lajos Kossuth, January 9, 1852, in *Collected Works*, 2:115–16; for Mexico, see Jay Monaghan, *Diplomat in Carpet Slippers: Abraham Lincoln Deals with Foreign Affairs* (Indianapolis: Bobbs-Merrill, 1945), esp. 401–3.

Had Lincoln not existed, had he been less than he was, or had the battle to keep the nation together been lost, it would have meant the end of the American experiment. Secession would have bred secession, reducing us into smaller and smaller fragments with disintegration inevitable. The miracle would have been killed in its infancy. Lincoln saved us from that. But in having won the first great war for unity, he did not relieve us from the need to fight the further battles of balancing our diversity with our harmony, of keeping the pieces of the mosaic intact while making room for new pieces both here at home and abroad. And we must fight to assure that our nation does not become a society of sharply disparate economic classes where disproportionate shares of the nation's abundance are directed to the already fit and fortunate while the rest are ignored or despised.

Lincoln believed with every fiber of his being that this place, America, could offer an achievable dream to all mankind that was different than any other in the annals of history. A dream that was more generous, more compassionate, and more inclusive. He would have known that we cannot end terror in the world just by having the world's most powerful weapons and best fighting force anymore than we can end crime in America only by having the best police and prisons. We have to add to this force whatever is needed to provide the realistic hope for opportunity and dignity that quiets rage and produces peace.

Lincoln's belief in the American people and the inspiration we can provide the rest of the world was broader, deeper, and more daring than any other person's of his age—and perhaps, of ours, too. With that belief he not only led us, he created us. His personal mythology became our national mythology. Lincoln embodied his age in his actions and in his words. Words even and measured—calling us to our destiny. Words he prayed and troubled over—more than a million words in his speeches and writings. Words that chronicled the search for his own identity as he searched for a nation's identity as well. Words ringing down into the present. Words that argued for the belief that the promise must be kept—that the dream must endure and grow until it embraces everyone.

We do indeed need something real to believe in and hold on to. Something sweeter than the taste of a political victory, something stronger and grander that can help us deal with our problems by making us better than we are instead of meaner. Something that can lift our aspirations instead of lowering them. This book was designed to help us find this something by using Lincoln as he should be used.

Great challenges remain for our country and for the world. As the richest nation in the world we have only our own lack of political will to blame for the large number of Americans who are unemployed, poor, not properly cared for when ill, or struggling not to slide backward economically. Lincoln's message to us is clear. He calls upon us to meet those challenges by going forward, painful step by painful step, to enlarge the greatness of this nation with "patient confidence in the ultimate justice of the people" here in our still imperfect Union.[5] And then—he tells us—it is our destiny to spread that gift of equality and unity to the rest of the world—to Afghanistan, to Iraq, to Africa and everywhere!

---

5. From the first inaugural address, March 4, 1861, in *Collected Works*, 4:270.

LINCOLN AS
POLITICAL SCRIPTURE

THE YEAR WAS 1992. The scene was the Republican National Convention in Houston, Texas. Republicans were about to renominate President George Bush for a second term and then return home to try convincing American voters that the nation's economic recession had little to do with the Republican Party, its philosophy, or its standard-bearer. The task must have seemed daunting. In the end it proved impossible, but for one brief moment the goal seemed within their grasp. That was when the much-loved former president, Ronald Reagan, arrived at the speaker's rostrum to rouse the faithful to a renewed dedication to modern Republican ideals.

He did so by invoking the name of Lincoln. Exhuming a credo that President Reagan told us had been "so eloquently stated" by Lincoln generations earlier, the fortieth president quoted what he described as four of Lincoln's most appealing maxims. Here was a hallowed set of principles, Reagan declared, that had stood the test of time and deserved to be recalled and repeated again and again to fortify America against a resurgent liberalism. To some people listening to Reagan that night, the phrases must have seemed crafted to rebut with uncanny specificity the rise of Governor William Jefferson Clinton of Arkansas. As the newly anointed Democratic challenger to twelve consecutive years of Republican White House rule and leading in all the public-opinion polls, Clinton posed a formidable threat to Reagan's conservative revolution. Now Reagan summoned all of his rhetorical gifts to remind the hundreds of delegates packing the convention hall and the tens of millions more watching on television that another Republican, Abraham Lincoln, had once wisely offered the following timeless truths:

> *You cannot strengthen the weak by weakening the strong.*
>
> *You cannot help the wage earner by pulling down the wage payer.*
>
> *You cannot help the poor man by destroying the rich.*
>
> *You cannot help men permanently by doing for them what they could and should do for themselves.*

The convention floor erupted in waves of applause. TV cameras captured the faces of emotional delegates whose nods of assent evidenced the deep understanding and gratitude one feels upon hearing a revered pastor deliver a grand sermon. Reagan had resurrected a tablet of political commandments more prescient and eloquent than any arid Republican Party platform or windy acceptance speech. No one had ever said it better than the Great Emancipator as revivified by the Great Communicator. It was a magical combination. As politics and performance, even liberal Democrats admitted that it was good.

As it turned out, it was indeed too good to be true.[6] In fact, Lincoln had never uttered a word of it. The lines turned out to be the work of an obscure German-born, Brooklyn-ordained minister named William John Henry Boetcker, and they dated back to only 1916—fifty-one years after Lincoln's death. That year, Boetcker published a tract entitled *Lincoln on Private Property*. The pamphlet featured a unique format: the true words of Lincoln on one page followed by interpretive quotations from Boetcker on the next. The ideas quickly found an appreciative audience among conservatives. Republican clubs clamored for copies, and the booklet went into new editions in 1917, 1938, and 1945. Unfortunately, in each subsequent incarnation Boetcker progressively receded into the background until Lincoln was receiving sole and undeserved credit for aphorisms he had never uttered. One later edition boasted that the words were Lincoln's exclusively and were published at the "inspiration of William J. H. Boetcker." By the time Ronald Reagan got around to quoting these lines, the true source of the inspiration had faded into the shadows. When the truth finally surfaced, a Reagan spokesman, scrambling for an explanation, said that the former president had done all his own research. As the sole author of the speech he had found the "Lincoln" quotations in a book called *The Toastmaster's Treasure Chest* by one Herbert V. Prochnow. It was passed off as an understandable mistake, but it is an indelible one.[7]

---

6. See Gabor S. Borrit, ed., *Of the People, By the People, For the People and Other Quotations from Abraham Lincoln* (New York: Columbia University Press, 1996), 144–45.
7. Herbert Mitgang, "Reagan Put Words in Lincoln's Mouth," *The New York Times*, August 19, 1992, A-13.

Few of the millions who heard Reagan that summer night ever read the explanations or the corrections published in newspapers during the days following his remarks. Nor did they learn that with a brilliant editorial stroke, Reagan had craftily omitted two of those spurious Boetcker-authored quotes—two that did not seem to fit his call for fealty to Republican principles 1992-style. After all, how could the chief executive who had presided over the accumulation of the most massive federal deficit and debt in the nation's entire history possibly say:

You cannot keep out of trouble by spending more than your income.

You cannot establish security on borrowed money.

Ronald Reagan deleted those phrases from his recitation. But he had said enough to lay powerful, if spurious, claim to Lincoln's political blessings. Three full years after scholars had discredited Reagan's Houston Lincoln reference, one of the most widely read newspaper columnists in the nation blithely published the Boetcker quotes once again. To Ann Landers, the words Reagan had quoted still seemed irresistibly Lincolnian.[8]

Claiming the mantle of Lincoln started long before President Reagan's faux pas. It has been part of the fabric of political discourse practically from the moment Lincoln was assassinated on Good Friday, 1865—barely a week after restoring peace to a country torn by the long, blood-soaked Civil War. In eulogies delivered at churches throughout the north that Easter Sunday, Lincoln was confirmed as a secu-

---

8. Ann Landers column, published in the *Gettysburg Times*, July 26, 1995.

lar saint. That was a nearly miraculous elevation for one who was among the most severely criticized of all of our presidents: Lincoln had been mocked, scorned, and ridiculed by much of the nation until he was lifted above the clamor by his martyrdom. Gone was the hateful derision. To many, he had suddenly become a second Moses, proclaiming liberty throughout the country but perishing before he could enjoy the promised land; to others, he was an American savior dying for the sins of his bitterly divided people.[9]

Before long, politicians took up where preachers had left off. In the furious debate over postwar Reconstruction, conservatives and so-called radicals both claimed they were pursuing the path to reconciliation that Lincoln himself had charted. Then at the dawn of the twentieth century, Democrats like William Jennings Bryan began suggesting that they, too, might be entitled to claim a portion of Lincoln's legacy. An angry *New York Times* article replied that "every word of that noble man ought to be a rebuke" to such Democratic presumption, but the indignation of the *Times* did nothing to inhibit the Democrats.[10] Lincoln's reputation, buoyed by the centennial observances of his birth, remained high; and competition to claim Lincoln for political inspiration and advantage came to embrace all political faiths. A golden age of Lincoln literature was just getting underway, and politicians were eager to lay claim to its riches. It would have been unnatural for politicians *not* to clamber aboard the bandwagon.

---

9. See, for examples, Thomas Reed Turner, *Beware the People Weeping: Public Opinion and the Assassination of Abraham Lincoln* (Baton Rouge, LA: Louisiana State University Press, 1982), 77–89.

10. Merrill Peterson, *Lincoln in American Memory* (New York: Oxford University Press, 1994), 158.

Theodore Roosevelt, who as a child had viewed Lincoln's funeral procession in New York City, proudly confided to White House correspondents that he kept a portrait of Lincoln behind his presidential desk. "When I am confronted with a great problem," he explained. "I look up to that picture, and I do as I believe Lincoln would have done." Roosevelt felt comfortable pursuing what he called a "Jackson-Lincoln theory of the presidency," meaning that he would be an active executive prepared to do even what Congress was reluctant to approve. Lincoln, Teddy Roosevelt claimed, had practiced "tempered radicalism," and so would he. By then the competition to claim Lincoln had come to embrace all political faiths. By the time the 1912 election rolled around, Democrat Woodrow Wilson felt compelled to establish an association of his own with the great Lincoln. Explaining that he was in search of the unique inspiration Lincoln could provide, the Democratic nominee even made a pilgrimage to the sacred and hitherto exclusively Republican mecca of Springfield, Illinois, Lincoln's hometown.[11]

The Democrat who worked most assiduously of all to seize the Lincoln legacy was Franklin Delano Roosevelt. As governor of New York, Roosevelt admitted to a newspaperman that one of his goals was for "us Democrats to claim Lincoln as one of our own." With characteristic zeal and deftness, Roosevelt proceeded to do precisely that. In 1932 he attempted what no member of his party had done since the passage of the Fourteenth Amendment gave African Americans the franchise—he competed successfully for the black vote, which had always been rock solid for the party of Lin-

11. Merrill, *Lincoln in American Memory*, 160, 164.

coln. Once in the White House, he freely quoted Lincoln to justify New Deal initiatives. Woodrow Wilson had journeyed to Springfield. Franklin Delano Roosevelt stepped further back into time and myth; he traveled to Lincoln's log cabin birthplace in Kentucky. Before long, the Democrat Roosevelt had convinced Americans that no politician had more in common with the onetime prairie rail-splitter than the squire of Hyde Park, thereby, according to historian Michael Kammen, "de-politicizing American party history." By the dawn of World War II, most Americans had come to believe that Roosevelt and Lincoln "represented a prominent line of continuity in American leadership."[12] There was good reason for that; both men had successfully led America through great crises and helped to define the democratic character of the first great democratic nation.

The eagerness of our leaders to seek Lincoln's guidance and blessing has continued unabated ever since. In the 1950s, it was Illinois Democrat Adlai E. Stevenson who leaned heavily on Lincoln. In Stevenson's view, Lincoln, much like Stevenson himself, would have advocated strong American leadership around the globe. The two-time Democratic presidential nominee suggested that Lincoln's words offered "a call to *a new battle*—a battle which rages around us now in every part of the world in this new time of testing."[13]

12. Michael Kammen, *Mystic Chords of Memory: The Transformation of Tradition in American Culture* (New York: Alfred A. Knopf, 1991), 294, 452; see also *New York Times,* February 12, 1935, 10; February 13, 1935, 23.

13. Stevenson's speech, "Unfinished Work of Emancipation," was delivered at the Lincoln Memorial in Washington, D.C., on September 18, 1962. See Waldo C. Braden, ed., *Building the Myth: Selected Speeches Memorializing Abraham Lincoln* (Urbana: University of Illinois Press, 1990), 224.

Lyndon Johnson and Richard Nixon both aggressively identified themselves with Lincoln doctrine, especially in wartime. Besieged by critics, they took to comparing their suffering and isolation to Lincoln's, portraying themselves as heirs to his legacy of hunkering down and fighting on, even in the wake of dwindling popularity at home and declining fortunes on the battlefields of Southeast Asia. Nixon even made sure he was photographed "relaxing"—sitting in an easy chair in a fully-buttoned black suit—beneath a comforting lithograph of Lincoln and his family at the White House.[14]

In the 1990s, Republicans like Jack Kemp weighed in, seeking to associate their supply-side programs with the political philosophy of the sixteenth president. Lincoln, they argued, was at heart much like themselves, an unapologetic economic conservative. Meanwhile, President Bill Clinton kept a bust of Lincoln behind his Oval Office desk, where it was prominently visible during White House addresses. On a nearby table stood a small statuette of Lincoln and Douglas in debate. Clinton read new Lincoln books, quoting him periodically, and enthusiastically assembled a White House collection of original editions of every old book Lincoln had ever read as a youth.

On Lincoln's birthday in 1998, Speaker of the House Newt Gingrich suggested in a provocative, widely reported speech that any student of Lincoln would conclude that

---

14. See Harold Holzer's "White House Lincolniana: The First Family's Print of the Lincolns," *The Lincoln Herald* 76 (Fall 1974): 119–31.

America must bomb Iraq. "To do less," he said, "would be to betray the very cause of freedom that was at the heart of Lincoln." In the end, America did not bomb Iraq, leaving the imagined "heart of Lincoln" to be invoked again in the future.[15]

George Herbert Walker Bush professed admiration for Lincoln as well. After winning the Gulf War, he suggested that his official portrait show him standing before a White House painting of Lincoln with his military chiefs at their final council of war in 1865—complete with a symbolic rainbow breaking out on the horizon to presage the return to peace. Bush posed so that his own face discreetly covered Lincoln's, but the unspoken suggestion of identification with Lincoln was hard to mistake.[16]

The second President Bush also counts himself as an admirer of Lincoln. Like his predecessor, he keeps a portrait of Lincoln in the Oval Office and, despite the demands on his time, keeps up with Lincoln literature. "I've got Lincoln's picture on the wall here," he told a journalist in 2003, "because I am reminded that I must work to unite the country, which Lincoln understood, to achieve great goals." Interestingly, the same painting that inspired the father fascinates—and worries—his son. In early 2004, President Bush confided to a

---

15. Newt Gingrich, "Abraham Lincoln: The Centrality of the Declaration of Independence," address to the Claremont Institute's Lincoln Day Symposium, Washington, D.C., February 12, 1998, reprinted in *Vital Speeches of the Day*.

16. The painting is the *Peacemakers* by G. P. A. Healy. See Harold Holzer, "The Return of the Peacemakers: The Great Emancipator and the Liberator of Kuwait Are Together in the Newest White House Portrait," *American Heritage* 47 (February–March 1996): 68–69.

group of visitors that the *Peacemakers* portrait showed how presidents age under the strain of leading a nation through war.[17]

Earlier, President Bush chose to welcome home veterans of the Iraq war by landing on the flight deck of the aircraft carrier USS *Abraham Lincoln*. Predictably, the old Democrat warhorse Senator Robert C. Byrd of West Virginia promptly denounced the event, noting: "As I watched the president's fighter jet swoop down onto the deck . . . I could not help but contrast the reported simple dignity of President Lincoln at Gettysburg with the flamboyant showmanship of President Bush aboard the USS *Abraham Lincoln*."[18]

Just days before the March 2004 New York Democratic presidential primary, Senator John Edwards of North Carolina became the latest—though undoubtedly not the last—White House aspirant to cite Lincoln.

Asked if he believed "God is on America's side" in President Bush's war on terrorism, Edwards recalled "a wonderful story about Abraham Lincoln during the middle of the Civil War, bringing in a group of leaders, and at the end of the meeting one of the leaders said, 'Mr. President, can we . . . please join in prayer that God is on our side?' And Abraham Lincoln's response was, 'I won't join you in that

17. "Bush: In His Own Words," *U.S. News & World Report* (December 30, 2002–January 6, 2003): 22; *New York Times*, March 7, 2004. Karl Rove, a key White House aide, is a well-read Lincoln admirer who invites historians to deliver lectures for the senior staff and keeps Civil War–era memorabilia on his own office wall, including the influential 1866 engraving, *First Reading of the Emancipation Proclamation before the Cabinet.*

18. "Making the Military a Prop in Presidential Politics," address by Senator Robert C. Byrd before the United States Senate, May 2003, from the transcript on the senator's Web site, http://byrd.senate.gov/

prayer, but I'll join you in a prayer that we're on God's side.'" The winner of the primary, Senator John Kerry of Massachusetts, had the last word. Claiming victory, he reminded supporters that heavenly guidance notwithstanding, what remained important was that Lincoln believed America to be "the last best hope of earth."[19]

And so Lincoln once again became a measuring stick for presidential performance, and as the pivotal presidential election year of 2004 arrived, candidates from both parties prepared to begin the quadrennial struggle over the right to the Lincoln legacy. That could have been a great blessing.

This chapter was written with Harold Holzer.

19. Transcript of the CBS-*New York Times* debate, on http://query.nytimes.com/abstract.html; Kerry remarks, March 2, 2004, from http://www.johnkerry.com/pressroom/speeches/spc_2004_0302.html.

LINCOLN'S WISDOM
FOR TODAY

WHAT IS IT ABOUT Abraham Lincoln that makes him an iconic figure to politicians with all sorts of ideologies? He was one of the most severely criticized of all our presidents. In the only one of his two electoral victories in which the entire nation voted, he did not get a majority vote—in fact, he received less than 40 percent. He was mocked, scorned, and ridiculed by much of the country until he was lifted above the clamor by his assassination, and pockets of detractors still castigate him today as either a racist or a tyrant whose dominant trait as president was his muted arrogance.

Even ardent admirers acknowledge his manifest imperfections: his ambition, his law partner conceded, was like "a little engine that knew no rest."[20] He could be a devious and supple politician with a Machiavellian cunning. He had a mixed record of disappointment and success as a lawyer and a politician. His family life was often distressing and trouble-ridden, and he was vulnerable to fits of melancholy. He had little formal education and scant experience as an executive

---

20. William H. Herndon, *Herndon's Lincoln: The True Story of a Great Life*, 3 vols. (orig. pub. 1889; Springfield, Ill.: Herndon's Lincoln Publishing Co., n.d.), 2:375.

before his one and only full term as president, and his first year in office—which brought the nation into a civil war—can hardly be characterized as auspicious. As one historian has asserted, had Lincoln been assassinated in 1861 instead of in 1865 he would long ago have been relegated to the dustbin of history.[21]

On the other hand, Lincoln was gifted with a dazzling array of admirable personal attributes and a fortuitous combination of circumstances that gave him an opportunity that he seized to achieve greatness.

Lincoln's humble beginnings as the descendant of immigrants and pioneers made him a natural favorite of the generations of seekers and strugglers who have built this nation and continue to strengthen it. His high intelligence, powerful sense of practicality, elegant speeches and writings, and his general deportment—which created an impression of rock-solid honesty, integrity, and strength wrapped in a charming, soft persona—added to his attractiveness.

The Civil War, the greatest internal threat ever posed to our nation's existence, gave him the opportunity to demonstrate greatness as a thinker, writer, speaker, and leader. He made the most of that opportunity by both preserving the Union and initiating the process that ended slavery.

It took an extraordinary leader and politician to do all that he did, one that cannot be adequately defined by the usual political descriptions so popular today. As President John F. Kennedy pointed out, we can't fully understand contemporary problems if we are bound by the traditional labels

---

21. Mark E. Neely, Jr., "Lincoln and Liberty," in Mario M. Cuomo and Harold Holzer, eds., *Lincoln on Democracy* (New York: HarperCollins, 1990), 237.

and worn-out slogans of an earlier era. Kennedy would be dismayed today to know that despite his admonition, the problem of simplistic sloganeering and the pandering use of stereotypes is worse in this electronic age than it was four decades ago. It was also a problem in Lincoln's time, but not one to which he contributed. Lincoln's unique intellectuality, cogency, and subtlety manifested themselves in his thoughtful and substantive approach to issues. If he made a place for rough generalizations, it was certainly not first place—that he reserved for common sense and reasonableness. Over the years, analysts and historians have occasionally resorted to one-word descriptions of Lincoln, like J. G. Randall's references to him as a great liberal and President Reagan's insistence that Lincoln was surely a conservative like himself. The truth is, Lincoln was too large, complex, and grand to be captured by any of those shopworn rhetorical labels.

A close look shows that Lincoln was on occasion a wily and grittily pragmatic politician in the conduct of his presidential duties—even when dealing with constitutional principles. Like FDR he often claimed the end justified the means. Stepping back, however, and viewing him in a larger context, we are dazzled by the dimensions of his intelligence and the strength of his will. The Lincoln scholar Frank J. Williams, chief justice of the Supreme Court of Rhode Island, made a point of how much broader and deeper Lincoln's intellectual reach was when he noted that Lincoln raised important and fundamental questions. Like Socrates, who put Athens on trial, Lincoln put America on trial, testing our nation's commitment to the ideals of the Declaration of Independence during the Civil War. Through his unbending determination, political skill, and capacity to inspire, he was able to put this nation back together after it had come apart, making it stronger than it was by elevating the moral stature of the Union to a level of equality, civility, and fairness that the Declaration of Independence had hoped for but that the Founding Fathers doubted was possible.

The accomplishments made Lincoln the mythic and majestic figure that he is today and assured him a place on the top tier of the pantheon of American political heroes along with George Washington and Franklin Delano Roosevelt. Washington is revered as the nation's father who launched the spectacular journey of American democracy; Franklin Delano Roosevelt's leadership helped us through the excruciating challenges of the Great Depression and the Second World War. Lincoln not only saved the nation from fragmentation but also enriched our democratic character by adding to our constitutional guarantee of liberty the even higher aspiration and promise of the Declaration of Independence—the inalienable right to equality.

Of these three great presidents, Lincoln has been by far the one most consulted and leaned on for advice and affirmation. This is because, in addition to his unique accomplishments, which the nation will celebrate forever, Lincoln left us an invaluable legacy of ideas, principles, and vision. Perhaps his greatest gift to us was the lofty grandeur, soundness, and durability of the wisdom he communicated to the nation and the world.

We need that wisdom today more than ever. Despite all the wealth and grandness so apparent in our great land, it is not clear that we know exactly what we want to be as a nation. Despite our unrivaled military and economic strength, we are unsure whether we should be the planet's imperious dominator or its supportive, uplifting, and unifying democratic inspiration. We have suddenly lost international credibility and become more isolated than at any time in recent history. We hunger for larger, better answers than we are receiving from our leaders. Lincoln can help us find those answers. During the years after his martyrdom, his voice has remained as true and clear as a great church bell, reminding us how much better this nation and world would be if only we listened and learned. Lincoln speaks today not only to his own countrymen but also to his brothers and sisters worldwide. He does it with timeless words that may be the most eloquent an American political figure has ever produced. It is little wonder that ambitious politicians claim him as their inspiration, that studious politicians seek his guidance, and that audacious politicians seek his imprimatur. Shouldn't we be equally interested in measuring our potential decisions against those he might have made?

There are, of course, cautions to observe. In measuring these decisions we must keep in mind the differences in context. Even with his lively imagination and interest in things mechanical, Lincoln could not have foreseen the complex tapestry of high-tech problems that his White House heirs confront. Lincoln had no hint of atomic bombs, space travel, human cloning, or images and sounds being flashed instantly from continent to continent. Nevertheless, the breadth, width, and depth of his wisdom penetrate through the surface of many temporal issues into the heart of matters modern and seemingly insoluble. For as Lincoln recognized: "The struggle of today is not altogether for today; it is for a vast future also."[22]

It appears Lincoln may have expected us to look back at his accomplishments. "The fiery trial through which we pass," he declared nine months after taking office, "will light us down, in honor or dishonor, to the latest generation." Facing the greatest crisis in the nation's history, he drew inspiration from the nation's founders and their determination years before his own presidency began to hallow the notion that all men are created equal. To Lincoln, those maxims represented an "electric cord" that ennobled the present and illuminated the future.[23]

Surely Lincoln would agree that this original promise remains today the unfinished work of the nation and that he would want to lend a hand in achieving it. In a small way this book gives us the opportunity to avail ourselves of his offer by exploring his views as we search for answers to today's challenges. He belongs to all of us, and we should use him. Perhaps FDR, the closest president to Lincoln we have ever elected to the White House since, said it best when he launched his bid for a third term by declaring:

> I do not know which party Lincoln would belong to if he were alive [today] . . . I am more interested in the fact that he did the big job which then had to be done—to preserve the Union and make possible the

---

22. From the first annual message to Congress, December 3, 1861, in *Collected Works*, 5:53.

23. From a speech in Chicago, July 10, 1858, in ibid., 2:500.

united country that we all live in today. His sympathies and his motives of championship of humanity itself have made him for all centuries to come the legitimate property of all parties—of every man and woman and child in every part of our land.[24]

BEFORE GOING BACK in time and calling on Lincoln directly, I want to describe briefly in the next chapter the nation's condition as I see it on the brink of the presidential election of 2004. While I make no claim to be a historian, I have been an ardent and dutiful student of the great Lincoln since my days in college—long before I even considered the possibility of a political career. What appealed to me most about Lincoln was not his humble background, his accomplishments, or even his magnificent eloquence, but his lucidity, the sureness of his logic, the cogency of his analysis, and the apparent reasonableness of his conclusions. In my days as a college student, a law student, a lawyer, and then a professor, Lincoln made good sense to me most of the time. Apparently that's how judges and juries felt about him as well because he rose to the top rank of courtroom lawyers in Illinois. That clean and compelling intelligence also manifested itself in his major speeches, perhaps most notably in his fa-

---

24. Speech at the Jackson Day dinner, January 8, 1940, in Samuel I. Rosenman, ed., *The Public Papers and Addresses of Franklin D. Roosevelt*, 13 vols. (New York: Random House, 1938), 9:29–30. The best recent comparison of the two presidents is Ronald D. Reitveld, "Franklin D Roosevelt's Abraham Lincoln," in William D. Pederson and Frank J. Williams, eds., *Franklin D. Roosevelt and Abraham Lincoln: Competing Perspectives on Two Great Presidents* (Armonk, NY: M.E. Sharpe, 2003), 10–60.

mous Cooper Union address in New York in 1860—a speech that accelerated his progress on the path to the presidency. I am sure that as a result of my admiration, many of the views I express were shaped directly or indirectly by Lincoln's writings and actions, and most of my ideas are consistent with his views as I understand them. A few of my views disagree with Lincoln's conclusions, perhaps because of my misunderstanding of his positions or simply because even the wisest president will not be able to convince all of his constituents all of the time.

TODAY'S AMERICA:
AN UNFINISHED WORK

OVERALL I SUSPECT that Lincoln would have been gratified at how far we have come but disappointed that we have not come far enough. Today we are the mightiest nation in the world with the largest economy and most powerful array of military forces and weapons. We have the benefit of good climate, water, and exemplary human resources from all parts of the world. We have proven to be the greatest engine of opportunity ever, giving generations of people from other lands a chance to succeed that they would not have had in their land of origin. Thanks in great part to our nation's success, democracy has become the most desirable form of government worldwide. Twice in the last century we helped save the world from calamitous tyranny and are now in a struggle to end international terrorism.

If our only ambition as a nation were to become the most successful and strongest nation in the world, we could relax our efforts immediately, at least until China or some combination of other nations caught up. The challenges for us now are how to make more of our vast potential than we already have and how to help the rest of the world experience the kind of success we have enjoyed.

Our domestic progress is uneven. We are the wealthiest nation in the world, boasting of more billionaires, millionaires, and people earning over $200,000 a year than any other country. This is an emphatic affirmation of the potential of free enterprise, but less than 2 percent of all Americans are doing that well in this increasingly and troublesomely fragmented society. By the end of the Clinton administration 22 million new jobs had been created, unemployment had declined, the middle class and poor were moving up the economic ladder, and the nation was enjoying its largest budget surplus in history. All of that has changed dramatically. Today our economy is nearly 70 percent consumption with the American people as its main consumers. But their consumption is limited by their relatively low income and extraordinarily high debt. Most of us are not poor enough to receive public assistance, but we are not doing well enough to be free of constant worry and agitation, either. Only one in five of our 140 million workers can be called highly skilled. The rest, their productivity hobbled by a lack of adequate education and training, earn modest incomes and their living conditions are worsening. The median household income is about $42,000 and goes up only about 1 percent a year while the costs of health care, education, transportation, and housing are increasing much faster than that. Many Americans are already up to their ears in credit-card and mortgage debt. Consumer debt for the average family has tripled in just one generation, and another record for personal bankruptcies was set last year as a result.

Nearly 3 million jobs have been lost in the last few years, and some 15 million American workers are unemployed, not looking for work, or working only part-time because they cannot find a full-time job. It seems inevitable that President Bush's tenure will record the worst job creation performance in modern history.

Economists agree that the recent economic resurgence after the beginning of the last short recession that began in March of 2001 and ended that November was not the result of a sudden and enduring increase in the wealth of American worker-consumers. It had more to do with importing foreign workers, exporting work to skilled employees in India or less-skilled employees in China and Mexico, or getting more production out of our own workers without paying significant additional compensation. Without new and better jobs to generate increased income for our worker-consumers, they will be hard-pressed to keep up their spending.

Overall, the recovery of early 2004 is a reflection of growing economic bifurcation—the stock market, corporations, luxury retailers, and investment bankers are all doing markedly better. Most Americans, however, are not. Nearly half of all American families now own shares of stock, but they own only a few thousand dollars' worth. They depend upon wages to live, and wages are not growing appreciably for those lucky enough to have jobs.

A huge trade deficit that receives little attention from the great mass of Americans is also a long-term threat to our economy even as it offers American consumers low-cost goods. The trade deficit now exceeds 5 percent of our GDP, cheapening our dollar, increasing our dependence on foreign investments, and inviting higher interest rates.

And with health-care costs soaring out of reach, more than 43 million Americans don't qualify for Medicaid, are not old enough for Medicare, or are not lucky enough to have a health insurance plan. This means that a worker suffering a serious illness—a woman struck by breast cancer, or a man suffering with prostate cancer for example—may receive treatment but will be bankrupted because she or he cannot afford to pay for it.

LINCOLN WOULD SURELY be disappointed if he took the measure of what he described at Gettysburg in 1863 as America's "unfinished work." In effect, much of America is struggling to avoid sliding back down the mountain, and many Americans have not yet started their ascent. Hunger and homelessness are on the rise in our major cities. In this, the richest nation in the world, nearly 35 million Americans live in poverty, 11 million of them children at risk of inadequate education, joblessness, and abuse of all kinds. Many of them grow up in neighborhoods surrounded by pimps, prostitutes, drugs, and violence. Some grow up familiar with the sound of gunfire before they have even heard an orchestra play. Without improved schools, housing, and more and better jobs, they will probably wind up tragic human failures, and their lack of productivity will continue to be a drag on the economy.

Although there are no totally reliable records, it is estimated that more than 8 million, perhaps even as many as 12 million, of our current residents are undocumented aliens, saddled with all the pressures and threats their lack of legitimacy produces.

All these problems are increasingly difficult to deal with today because of the huge and growing federal budget deficit and debt, already, in absolute numbers, the largest in our history, hanging like a great albatross around Uncle Sam's neck. The official federal debt is now more than $6 trillion. That is added to the approximately $45 trillion gap between anticipated costs and anticipated revenues needed to pay our projected Medicare and Social Security bills. Those mind-boggling numbers will be made even more enormous by the Republican-sponsored Medicare overhaul in 2003 that takes effect in 2006.

Adding to the fiscal burden are state and local deficits that in 2003 mounted to about $100 billion and produced unavoidable local tax increases and job losses. Unlike the federal government, local governments are mandated to balance their budget; they cannot simply print money, as Washington does, to keep up with the deficits and debt. The Federal Reserve has warned that eventually the federal deficits and debt will drive up interest rates, and a significant increase in interest rates would inevitably further slow the growth in our economy.

The huge annual deficits also weaken our Medicare and Social Security funds that are already in jeopardy. The number of potential beneficiaries in the years ahead far exceeds the number of workers we will have available to pay the taxes that will supply benefits—unless we expand our current immigration quotas, increase our birth rate, or find American jobs for more Americans.

The 2001 tax cut and the ones that followed it surrendered more than $2.5 trillion of federal revenue, about 40 percent of this money going back to the richest 1 percent of taxpayers in America. It was adopted specifically on the presidential assurance that "we don't need the money." This tax cut was criticized at the time as fiscally and economically unwise by the *Economist*, the *Wall Street Journal*, and most experts who could count but were not politicians. They have all been proven correct. The only tax cuts that had a visibly positive effect on the economy were those that went to the middle class because the money was spent on increased consumption of goods and services. The trillion or so dollars that went to the top 1 percent served a political purpose more than an economic one because these wealthy taxpayers already had the money they needed to buy things.

Despite all of this, the administration's announced plans for managing the economy in early 2004 amounted to a virtual concession to those critics who claimed these policies were designed to favor corporate interests and the already fit and fortunate over the rest of America. Their proposals to reduce the huge budget deficits they had created left their tax cuts to the already wealthy untouched and added further tax cuts for those who can afford to buy health insurance. They also left intact millions of dollars in what the celebrated Republican senator John McCain and others have called "corporate welfare." The pain will be felt instead by poor Americans who can't afford to pay rent or buy the prescription drugs they need, and by military veterans, the unemployed, and workers and students who are desperate for the training and education needed to provide them with the skills required to find a reasonably good job in this increasingly competitive environment. All of these dependent Americans will be asked to sacrifice by taking cuts in the benefits they need and expect to receive.

For the most part, the Democrats in Congress have been dominated by the Republican majorities in both houses and have not been able to advance their own agenda beyond the rhetorical stage. How this will change after November 2, 2004, will depend in significant measure on whether or not the Democratic campaign offers America specific policy alternatives and a fairer and more productive vision than those delivered so far by the Republicans.

AMERICA'S GLOBAL ROLE

THE LONG LITANY of serious domestic concerns had been temporarily eclipsed in the public's consciousness on 9/11/01, when our world changed dramatically and what has been called the "all-out war against terrorism" was launched.

After that we became entangled in Afghanistan and Iraq, struggling with an occupation and an attempt at nation building that has raised serious questions about our own nation's leadership. The administration's current rationale for the war is that we are liberators saving the Iraqi people from oppression and helping them to build a new democracy for their own good and to discourage terrorism.

This rationale, however, was an afterthought. President Bush began the war telling the world that Saddam Hussein possessed weapons of mass destruction and was complicit with al-Qaeda and therefore posed an imminent threat to our nation. These assertions were largely discredited and were replaced by the "liberation" rationale in a dazzling display of political legerdemain. Many Americans were left believing that, even if the president had not deliberately deceived them, they were victimized by a grotesquely damaging presidential mistake.

Everyone agrees that ridding the world of Saddam Hussein's brutality was good, but there continues to be strong disagreement over how it has been done. So far our Iraqi experience has cost more than a thousand American lives, along with the lives of uncounted thousands of Iraqis and the expenditure of billions of dollars. It threatens to continue keeping thousands of our troops at risk overseas for years to come and to cost many billions of dollars more, unless other nations can be persuaded to join in the effort and share its financial and personal burdens. This was made difficult by President Bush's rejection of the strong admonition from many nations not to proceed against Iraq preemptively in the first place. On the other hand, the obvious unworkability of a permanent American occupation makes an eventual transition to an international interim force and an all-Iraqi government inevitable. By the end of 2003, there were signs that Germany and France were putting aside their earlier displeasure with the United States' decision to go to war by joining in the reducing of Iraqi debt to help stabilize the new government. That was a hopeful indication that some of our damaged diplomatic relations are being repaired.

At the moment, our increasingly interdependent world is plagued by war, more terrorism, the worldwide tragedy of AIDS, poverty, and environmental degradation. Amid untapped abundance, millions of human beings in the rest of the world are starving to death, being killed by disease, or slaughtering one another out of a desperation to seize the resources they have not been allowed to develop and share.

When one looks objectively at the unmet challenges, the apocalyptic threats, and the squandered opportunities looming all around us, it is difficult not to be concerned about why we have not made more of our opportunities, even as we rejoice at our good fortune in being Americans.

Most Americans believe we have wasted much of our strength in one way or another and are eager for leadership that achieves more of our own potential. Certainly they would not be satisfied with the kind of nation we had in our early period of primitive individualism when the federal government helped only the land barons and business magnates, arguing that in the long run this would benefit everyone. In those years many millions died for lack of medical care and tried to survive without adequate housing or education. Millions more, of course, were kept in slavery merely because they were of African descent, and women were treated with less than the dignity they deserved.

At our best, we have always insisted on elevating our nation onto the high ground of our best possibilities. That surely is what Lincoln did, and it is what happened seven decades ago in the Depression when Franklin Roosevelt lifted himself from his wheelchair to marshal the strength that was left in America and used it to lift the rest of the country from its knees by supplementing the market system; by using our wealth to create more wealth; by investing in people, helping them to help themselves; and encouraging mutuality through the WPA, unemployment insurance, workmen's compensation, Home Relief, Social Security, and the public schools. Roosevelt reached beyond our own borders to make intelligent mutuality a global reality through the United Nations and years of foreign aid. Led by Democratic and Republican presidents, we encouraged synergism and provided sharing here at home through the G.I. Bill, the interstate highway system, Medicare, Medicaid, civil rights, and the space program with its avalanche of dividends in research and technology. More recently, we demonstrated our willingness to share in the pursuit of national prosperity by redistributing our wealth dramatically to pay penance for the sins of a market system that needed more discipline than it had received when we created the Resolution Trust Corporation and bailed out the savings and loan depositors.

These were good things to do, not just because they were compassionate but because they were intelligently pragmatic—like the Marshall Plan with which, despite the Holocaust and the murderous history of the Nazis and the Japanese warriors, we brought both nations back to life with billions of our dollars. There were many in my old neighborhood whose brothers, husbands, or fathers never came back from the war and who were not happy about what we were doing after it ended. But our nation helped these countries because we needed Europe and Japan as trading partners and we wanted to avoid the chaos that their postwar desperation might have created. We are doing the same thing for the same reasons in Russia today.

THE IMPACT OF President Bush's presidency has also been clearly evident in the new role religious issues are playing in our nation's political and cultural life. From the very inception of his administration the president has put a heavy emphasis on so-called faith-based policies and programs that are inspired by his own Christian religion. To a large extent, these programs have not been offensive to those with different religious beliefs; yet the role of religion in our society continues to be a source of controversy.

While most Americans tell pollsters they are religious and few politicians would openly champion atheism, religious differences often excite more distemper than equanimity. The Founding Fathers had predicted that difficulties would arise from competing religious views and had tried to reduce them by assuring both religious liberty and governmental neutrality in the Bill of Rights. Lincoln himself practiced that kind of fairness. He was the first commander in chief, for example, to commission non-Christian military chaplains—but that did not save him from being bitterly accused of being a nonbelieving heretic.

The predictions of difficulties created by religious differences were well founded. Some of the nation's most fiercely contentious debates on subjects like abortion, contraceptives, and stem-cell use can be traced in part to differing religious beliefs about when precisely life begins—a question that has engaged philosophers, religious thinkers, and scientists for ages. For example, President Bush's policies on abortion and stem-cell use are specifically predicated on his belief that human life begins with the fertilization of the egg. Nothing in the Declaration of Independence, the Constitution of the United States, our federal statutes, or our high-court rulings declares that to be the law; it is a purely religious tenet held by the president and millions of other Americans. As such, it appears to be far from the majority view; and despite this, the president has ruled against supporting the use of embryonic stem cells from thousands of unused embryos waiting to be destroyed because his firmly held religious belief would make that act equivalent to murder. That rationale also leads to the conclusion that no abortion, even to save the life of the mother, should ever be permitted—a view that was rejected by the Supreme Court in *Roe v. Wade* in 1973 and has been made the target of conservative presidents for three decades. It still is. President Bush has repeatedly suggested he would fill the first vacancy on the United States Supreme Court with someone who will vote with conservatives Clarence Thomas and Antonin Scalia to overrule *Roe v. Wade.* Democratic senators have responded with an equally rigid insistence that they will do everything possible to prevent the confirmation of such a candidate.

The struggle precipitated by differences over when life can be said to begin will undoubtedly continue for the foreseeable future. For now it appears the nation will continue the same pattern of dealing with the clash of religious and political questions already established in other areas, including the law concerning abortion. The right of true believers to live by their own religious beliefs will be guaranteed; no one will be compelled to use stem-cell research or its products, just as no one will be compelled to submit to an abortion. The nation will continue to respect the right of believers to advocate for changes in our civil law that correspond to their particular view of morality. But, as experience has shown, before this pluralistic nation will adopt these religious beliefs politically and make them the law of the land, the population will have to be persuaded by more than religious orthodoxy or the presumed authority of religious leaders.

With respect to abortion, as long as the belief that life begins at conception remains a minority view and there is no Constitutional amendment or Supreme Court ruling that defines life as beginning at conception, there will be no absolute ban on abortion. More likely is the possibility of a change in the law based on new medical evidence that moves the period of viability from twenty-four weeks as it is now established in *Roe v. Wade*, to a time earlier in pregnancy. In effect that will ban many abortions that are currently permitted. At the same time I expect there will be increased acceptance of policies and programs—for those whose religion permits them—like the ones I as governor and many others have promoted that seek to discourage unwanted pregnancies—sex education, birth-control instruction, facilitating the bringing of a fetus to term by providing poor women with at least the same benefits and help they would receive if they were choosing abortion, and enhancing the opportunities for adoption.

Whatever occurs, the controversies created by differences in religious convictions will continue to be a challenge to the nation's equanimity. They will surely test what Lincoln called "the better angels of our nature."[25]

---

25. Lincoln's first inaugural address, March 4, 1861, in *Collected Works*, 4:271.

TOWARD A BETTER AMERICA

WITH ALL OUR GLORIOUS history to guide us, what were we willing to do after 9/11 to perfect our Union? After passing nearly $2 trillion in tax cuts in 2001, we gave up still another huge portion of what the president called our "newly liberated wealth," bringing the total tax cut to more than $2.5 trillion. The largest piece, about $1 trillion, went to the smallest segment of our taxpayers and left our many domestic needs to be dealt with by the tender mercies of the market system.

Many Americans believed that instead of cutting taxes we should have begun a meaningful new effort to widen America's circle of opportunity by enhancing the productivity of those who are being left behind. We should have dealt with education, health care, and the environment instead of widening the gap farther between the already very successful and those still struggling. Domestic job creation should have been a priority in an attempt to replace the jobs being lost to lower-paid workers overseas. We should have remembered the fundamentals. Our 140 million workers are our principal potential consumers, and we should have invested more in improving their personal productivity, thereby increasing their ability to buy American goods and services.

The nation has been offered an inspirational lesson by the stunning contrast that came out of the horror of 9/11: the ugly and frightening reality of people who hated us so much that they were willing to give up their own lives to take ours was answered by the magnificent valor of hundreds of firefighters, policemen, emergency workers, and volunteers who loved humanity so much they were willing to risk their lives by charging into the smoke and flames in the hope that they might be able to save someone they did not even know.

That was a dramatic and ineffably beautiful reminder of the single most important principle we need to live by if we are to move upward toward a higher level of strength and civility. It is an idea as old as the idea of family that has moved us in our best moments to understand that the ability to increase our productivity and strength depends on how well we reconcile our profound instinct for individualism with the inescapable need for a sense of community.

We have seen the good effects of acting on that understanding over and over again for three-quarters of a century beginning with the Depression. We should have acted on it in 2001 and 2002 but failed to. We ought not to fail again.

There are many positive options available to us. We can make a new start by strengthening our whole nation, at the same time increasing our capacity to do more for the rest of the planet.

Here are some simple suggestions as to steps we could take immediately; many variations are possible.

We could defer 40 percent or so of the more than $2 trillion tax cuts that will go to the top earners in the country; that would make available approximately $1 trillion in resources.

Half of this revenue, $500 billion, could be used to reduce the deficit. The other half could be used in three ways. The first would be to create another stimulus to the economy by giving more tax relief to the consumers who are most likely to spend it because they have to. As already noted, the spurt in the economy in 2003 was produced largely by the tax rebates workers received earlier.

Another part of the redistributed tax cut could go to investments in the training, education, and health care we need to produce highly skilled workers and to care for those Americans we are not now reaching. One of our most serious problems is the loss of good jobs for Americans as globalization moves more of our production work to less-expensive, lower-skilled—and recently, even highly skilled—workers overseas. Rapidly enhancing worker productivity is reducing the number of higher-paying manufacturing jobs everywhere, exacerbating the problem of job loss.

Much of the political debate suggests that the answer is for our nation to move back toward the kind of protectionism that dominated the trade policy in Lincoln's time. That might increase the number of jobs available in the United States, but it would retard the economic growth of the poorer countries in the world who are now benefiting from their exports to us. In an ever more globalized world, what impoverishes many is bound to hurt us all. Certainly it would increase the already high level of hostility against us worldwide. A better idea is to use our already strong advantage in technology to increase the number of Americans working at what economist and former secretary of labor Robert Reich calls "symbolic analytic" work—doing research and development, design, engineering, high-level sales, marketing, and advertising. These workers include composers, writers, producers, lawyers, bankers, financiers, journalists, doctors, and management consultants. Most of the work will require more education and training than we have currently given 70 to 80 percent of our workers. Some of the trillion dollars we retrieve should be invested in providing that help. At the same time we should give readjustment assistance to workers who are losing their old jobs and get them ready for new ones, insist on fairer trade agreements like those we have with Canada and Australia, close loopholes that encourage the exporting of jobs, and provide incentives to keep jobs in America.

A third part of the revenue could go to state and local governments in the form of short-term revenue sharing so they can avoid the hurtful tax increases that we've seen in New York and many other states. We also need to defend ourselves at home. Our ports and the cargoes they receive need to be better monitored. There must be more effective scrutiny of passengers and baggage on trains, and we need to deal with the threat of shoulder-held missile launchers bringing down commercial airliners the way they bring down helicopters in Iraq. The unpreparedness of first responders, the lack of Arab-speaking intelligence agents, are obvious weaknesses that need to be addressed. These investments would also save jobs by avoiding layoffs of police officers, firefighters, and schoolteachers, and would increase employment by hiring the people needed for better homeland security.

A fourth piece of this revenue could go to additional investments in badly needed infrastructure work—another of our greatest requirements. This would also produce further job opportunities.

IT SEEMS CLEAR that we should be trying harder to realize Lincoln's vision of a nation that helps lift its people up the economic ladder and honors Americans' "right to rise." It is just as apparent that a similarly vigorous commitment to the idea of community and cooperation should guide us in using our power as a global hegemon.

We should stop pretending we can do what must be done without the help of much of the rest of the industrial world. Using up our wealth and sacrificing our young men and women to demonstrate our unique power as a nation is clearly not the way to win a global war against terrorism or increase world productivity.

Most disconcerting was the revelation in 2003 that there appeared to be no real strategy to fight terrorism. After wars in Afghanistan and Iraq that took thousands of lives and destroyed billions of dollars of vital infrastructure, a leaked memo from Secretary of Defense Donald Rumsfeld revealed that our government was not able to measure whether we had achieved any significant success in deterring terrorism. Even the dramatic capture of the brutal tyrant Saddam Hussein in December 2003, applauded by most of Iraq and the world as a step forward for civilization, did not produce a signal from the Department of Homeland Security's coded index that we were any safer than we had been before. Indeed, less than two weeks later the danger alert was raised to a level of higher urgency.

What then will it take to deter terrorism?

No one denies that some force is necessary and will continue to be required in order to deal with regimes and sovereignties that commit or support acts of terrorism. Individuals like Osama bin Laden and organizations like al-Qaeda are lethal tumors that must be destroyed. But as Israel's experience demonstrates, killing or apprehending terrorists will not rid us of the terrible cancer that created them.

On the other hand, if we were able to diminish or eradicate the motivations that trigger terrorism, we could deter more of it than we can with just our armies and munitions. It is estimated that a relatively small percentage of the 1.5 billion Muslims in the world are aggressively hostile toward the West, but their virulent propaganda, widely spread by satellite television and the Internet, is having a significant impact. Their hateful castigations go far beyond appeals to religious zealotry. Anti-Americanism and anti-Semitic conspiracy theories abound in the Arab and Muslim worlds, and a sophisticated and poisonous blend of fundamentalism and nationalism is used to foment violence against Western targets. Provocateurs condemn Western capitalism and its corrupting materialism that engenders social inequality in the Arab world. Realities past and current abet the message. A United Nations study says that in many of the countries with large Muslim populations, one in five people lives on less than two dollars a day and growth in income has been lower than anywhere else in the world except sub-Saharan Africa. This tremendous disparity with Western—especially American—affluence creates jealousy and resentment; and this antipathy is exacerbated by the perception in the Muslim world that the war against terrorism is being conducted against Muslims, not terrorists.

Our attack on Iraq exacerbated that hostility. In 2002 President Bush announced that Iran and North Korea were part of an "axis of evil" that included Iraq, then followed this statement with his new emphasis on "preemptive" war. This stunningly bellicose policy said we would start wars against people who we decided unilaterally might be a threat to our nation's well-being or even a threat to our hegemonic power.

Together with his earlier disavowal of a willingness to engage in "nation building" as a way to move the world toward greater democracy and his spurning of international compacts like the Kyoto Protocol and the Court of International Justice, the president's preemption statement made apparent his intention to lead the United States toward a new political aloofness—more unilateral and less willing to encourage new global cooperation and synergisms. After that, events apparently persuaded our president that his earlier inclinations were dangerous. Having miscalculated the difficulty of occupying, repairing, and redirecting the future of Iraq after defeating Saddam Hussein's army, the president was mollified and his belligerence with respect to North Korea and Iran was tempered. Instead of renewing the threat of preemptive war, Bush swallowed hard and began whispering gentler invitations to intelligent discussions and multilateral negotiations. He specifically rejected any intention to engage in attempted "regime changing" in Iran or North Korea, despite the continued suspicion that Iran was actually cooperating with terrorist organizations and the fact that both these members of the "axis of evil" posed nuclear threats to the rest of the world far more serious than those ever posed by Iraq. And in Iraq, the administration abandoned its previous rationale and supplanted it with the new "liberation through democracy" pledge.

This change in tactics was welcome. Better a chastened leader than a dangerously obstinate one. It remains clear, however, that better still would be a leader who would not need chastening to understand that the current hostility and terrorism cannot be undone with gunfire alone. Achieving what Lincoln called "peace with all nations" will require education, enlightenment, and substantial material support for the poorest areas of the Arab world in addition to the force of arms. With the significant assistance of as many partners as we can recruit, we need to complete our missions in Afghanistan and Iraq and help those millions of people to build their own free societies with strong economies, providing them the kind of opportunity many take for granted in the United States.

It has been obvious for a long time that removing our occupying troops from Iraq as soon as possible and leaving it up to the Iraqis to determine their own destiny as a free people are essential steps. Remember Lincoln: He knew when to wage war—and when to wage peace. After the conquest of Baghdad and the occupation by the coalition, Iraq became a gathering and festering place for all sorts of belligerent haters of the United States and for terrorists whose anger is being fed by the struggle with us as occupiers. The sooner we can leave the situation in the hands of the Iraqi people, the better.

We also must do better in the propaganda war that we are currently losing. Saudi Arabians and others who are supporting madrassas that teach Muslim youths to hate and kill the Western "infidels" must be stopped. Millions of people around the world believe that we Westerners are criminals, conspirators, and craven opportunists who exploit the down-trodden and callously ignore billions of the world's victims of oppression. Their minds will not be changed with tanks, missiles, or the fire from thousands of guns. We cannot run from the need to fight when it confronts us, but it is also true that we cannot intimidate our way to peace—we must instruct and inspire as well. Our mission should be to reach the world with a clearer view and understanding of the democratic principles we live by.

To do that well, we will have to assure that we do indeed continue to live by our principles. No matter how strong the temptation to put them aside under the pressure of war, zealous officials and judges should be discouraged from ignoring or distorting our Bill of Rights and the rule of law in the name of "security." Many Americans are concerned that the president's so-called Patriot Act allows his attorney general to keep his thumb on the scale when weighing the protections of the Bill of Rights against the need to protect the nation in time of war. In this regard, the attorney general's reliance on Abraham Lincoln's conduct during the Civil War suggests that the current administration intends to mimic some of Lincoln's most often challenged decisions concerning the applicability of the Bill of Rights.[26] If so, this would continue a regrettable pattern of suspension of constitutional prerogatives by presidents in time of war. The courts have generally tolerated these questionable assertions of authority by the executive branch of our government as

---

26. The standard reference on the subject is Mark E. Neely, Jr., *The Fate of Liberty: Abraham Lincoln and Civil Liberties* (New York: Oxford University Press, 1991).

long as the conflicts continued. Once the crises passed, constitutional normalcy has been restored. That was the case with the Japanese and the less-well-known Italian internments during the Second World War.

As of this writing, our Supreme Court has not yet had the opportunity to deal with the apparent excesses of the Patriot Act. In its haste to be politically correct, Congress appears to have threatened constitutionally guaranteed civil liberties by allowing secret searches of personal records—including library use, bookstore purchases, bank accounts, and medical histories—and by expanding the definition of terrorism to include the activities of advocacy groups that have nothing to do with the events of 9/11. Other dubious uses of presidential authority include the covert detention of 41,000 aliens; deportation hearings held in secret; and the requirement for visitors from other countries to register under threat of arrest, detention, and deportation. Even more egregious has been the arrest and detention of American citizens without a trial or access to a lawyer on the assumed authority of the president to declare an American an "enemy combatant" without having to justify or explain the designation. Federal circuit courts have challenged some of these decisions, but it is difficult to believe that the current conservatively oriented Supreme Court will overturn any of these administration decisions, especially since it is the court that virtually made Governor Bush president by its startling decision to accomplish by one vote what the nation had rejected at the polls by more than 500,000. It is more likely this Supreme Court will demonstrate the same predictable reluctance of past courts to challenge the wartime decisions of presidents.

On the other hand, hope springs eternal that one day soon a different Supreme Court will remember and respect the wisdom of an earlier decision in 1866. That year the Supreme Court retrospectively overturned the actions of President Abraham Lincoln who had effectively abolished the constitutional rights of dissenting American citizens during the Civil War. The Court said in *Ex parte Milligan*:

> No graver question was ever considered in this court, nor one which more nearly concerns the rights of the whole people; for it is the birthright of every American citizen when charged with crime to be tried and punished according to law. . . . The Constitution of the United States is a law for rulers and people, equally in war and in peace, and covers with the shield of its protection all classes of men, at all times and under all circumstances.
>
> No doctrine involving more pernicious consequences was ever invented by the wit of man than that any of [the Constitution's] provisions can be suspended during any of the great exigencies of government. Such a doctrine leads directly to anarchy or despotism, but the theory of necessity on which it is based is false; for the government, within the Constitution, has all the powers granted to it, which are necessary to preserve its existence.[27]

In later years other Supreme Court justices, pressured by world war, ignored the powerful legacy of *Ex parte Milligan*, but never repudiated the decision. We should remember the

---

27. *Ex parte Milligan*, 71 U.S. 2 (December 1866).

Supreme Court's words in *Milligan* today; we do not want to win the war against terrorism and then lose the peace by surrendering fundamental principles and freedoms that were, among other things, the target of terrorists whose own rigidly oppressive societies despise our liberty and the richness of life it has brought us.

Getting back onto a clear path upward toward a stronger and more civil United States will not be easy. We did not make a good start in nation building in Afghanistan or Iraq. We preemptively began a war that killed many of the people we claim to have wanted to liberate while also destroying much of their country. This did not engender a high degree of trust. Having launched the effort and lost the cooperation of many of our former major allies, we had no plausible way to retreat without making things worse. We were forced to go forward, hoping for better decisions along the way than those that brought us to this unhappy phase of our diplomatic history.

Dealing with the Israeli-Palestinian problem is also essential if we are to make any permanent progress. Justified or not, it may well be the single greatest cause of anger toward the United States in the Arab world and beyond. We must lead the peace effort together with Arab and other allies, with a new assertiveness that replaces the diffidence President Bush demonstrated in the beginning of his term and has returned to from time to time. It is essential we commit ourselves to an all-out effort to bring both sides together in a two-state solution with the same single-mindedness and aggressiveness that we demonstrated when Israel was created in 1948. Today, in addition to our concern for the victims of what appears to be perpetual undeclared warfare, 9/11 has given us a new and urgent self-interest—the violent struggle for survival and dignity between Israelis and Palestinians is now serving as a provocation to terrorists everywhere.

After the years of fighting, scheming, and negotiating, the elements of a settlement, although so far unachievable, are at least identifiable—two states living in mutual respect and divided essentially along their 1967 borders. This peaceful coexistence must be guaranteed by the world powers, who must assist both the Israelis and the Palistinians with all that is needed to build healthy economies, with educated, decently housed populations working together to make the desert bloom.

The United States needs to emphasize our desire for peace as powerfully and insistently as we have demanded an end to terrorism—especially since the two objectives are so tightly interwoven. Israel must agree to be flexible with respect to the land it has occupied after 1967. But, of course, the sine qua non to any workable settlement must be a sincere and effective effort by the Palestinians to end terrorism against Israel, as well as an unambiguously warranted acceptance of Israel's legitimacy by the Palestinians and the rest of the Arab world. It is a near absurdity to suggest that any final agreement can be made so long as significant Palestinian officials and other Arab leaders reserve the right to contest Israel's right to exist as a nation.

THERE IS MUCH MORE we must consider as we decide where we are going as a nation and how we can assure that the direction is upward toward completing the "unfinished work" identified by Lincoln. We have come a long way, but we still have a long way to go. No one would recognize that better than Lincoln, who did so much to bring us as far as we have come. With that in mind, let's look more closely at what Lincoln has to offer us by way of instruction regarding the challenges and opportunities before us today.

WHAT WOULD LINCOLN SAY?
War

PRESIDENT LINCOLN'S AND President George W. Bush's first months in office have a good deal in common. Both men were relatively unpopular choices, neither receiving even half the vote. And before the end of their first years, both were involved in wars that dominated their terms. Bush continues to be criticized by most Democrats for having initiated the war against Iraq and making a commitment to preemptive action whenever our nation believes itself threatened. The threat of Iraqi weapons of mass destruction never materialized and now appears never to have existed, so the president was forced to adopt a different rationale—"liberation through nation building"—which he had previously rejected but since has adroitly exploited.

It is still not clear how President Bush's war against terrorism will be judged by history. The terrorists' war will not be fought by nations and their armies but by zealots and their guerilla loyalists. Indeed, by its nature the war against terrorism is not a war that will end in a pact or a parade. It is more like the war against crime in that it will be ongoing with rising and falling intensity.

On the other hand, President Bush's new rationale will

provide a goal by which the struggle in Iraq will be separately measurable. The war will either succeed in creating a free nation led by a government that is fairly representative of its people and offers them economic opportunity in a market system or it will not. Only time will tell whether democracy or something less and worse prevails and what effect—if any—that will have on the terrorism that expressed itself on 9/11 with such devastating impact.

What will always be clear without waiting for the verdict of history is that the war in Iraq was a war we began because the president of the United States believed we had to, notwithstanding that much of the rest of the world and many in his own country disagreed.

Lincoln's situation was different, and so were his instincts.

The most famous wartime president in our history actually began his national political career as a peace advocate, opposed to an American war on foreign soil. Lincoln spoke out eloquently against America's conducting a foreign invasion even as he voted for appropriations bills designed to supply and arm the troops who conducted it. His delicately balanced position was unpopular enough back home in Illinois to lose him renomination for Congress, and for years, Lincoln's opposition to the Mexican War remained—to Democrats, at least—the soft spot in his political record. In a way, Lincoln was trying to have it both ways—scoring political points against the president of the opposite party, Democrat James Knox Polk, and taking political cover by supporting appropriations to fund the fighting he ostensibly opposed. But as Lincoln later insisted, "whenever there was an attempt to procure a vote of mine which would indorse [sic] the origin and justice of the war, I refused to give such indorsement, [sic] and voted against it." He continued to maintain that Mexico "was in no way molesting, or menacing the U.S.," while heaping lavish praise on the officers and men who fought on Mexican soil to "victory! victory!! victory!!!"[28]

During the Mexican War, Lincoln used his greatest eloquence on the House floor to warn against the intoxicating aura of war itself. It was a seductive exigency to be resisted, not pursued. People, he conceded, had "the right to rise up, and shake off the existing government," if it was oppressive. This was a "sacred right" that would ultimately "liberate the world." Lincoln never wavered where the right of an oppressed people to throw off the yoke of tyranny was concerned, but he remained opposed to intervention in foreign conflict without clear and provable justification. He insisted that even "national honor, the security of the future, [and] the prevention of foreign interference" could not justify the "fever-dream of war." He warned against "the exceeding brightness of military glory—that attractive rainbow, that rises in showers of blood—that serpent's eye, that charms to destroy."[29]

Lincoln's warnings proved to be prophetic in the Civil War. It was one of the most memorable, most significant, and bloodiest conflicts in our long history of wars. It was a terribly costly brother-against-brother "people's contest," led by Lincoln principally to prove, as he expressed it, that

---

28. Debate at Charleston, September 18, 1858, in *Collected Works*, 3:182; Autobiographical sketch for John L. Scripps, ca. June 1860, in ibid., 4:66; Eulogy for Zachary Taylor, July 25, 1850, ibid., 2:85.

29. Congressman Lincoln's speech on the Mexican War in the U.S. House of Representatives, January 12, 1848, in ibid. 1:439–40.

WHY LINCOLN MATTERS   •   63

"there can be no successful appeal from the ballot to the bullet."[30] He had to overcome growing antiwar sentiment within the North, an opposition party determined to restore peace even if it meant dividing up the United States, and the frightening threat that European powers might take advantage of the rebellion to launch their own war against America. The war cost the nation more than a million dead and wounded.

Apparently Lincoln himself, to some extent, fell victim to the "fever-dream of war," "the exceeding brightness of military glory," and the "serpent's eye that charms to destroy" once the South began the hostilities.

In a third-person autobiographical sketch he wrote for his 1860 presidential campaign, Lincoln remembered that as an eight-year-old frontier boy, he had shot a wild turkey one day and was so traumatized by the experience that he "never since pulled a trigger on any larger game." A great deal changed on his way to adulthood and a wartime presidency during which he once dismissed newspaper praise by noting cold-bloodedly, "Breath alone kills no rebels."[31] Lincoln knew that only weapons killed rebels, and once he became president, he was swept up in a relentless quest to acquire and place into service the most effective weapons he could secure. Even seeing the most horrifying casualties of war with his own eyes failed to dissuade him from his search for new technologies that he thought could shorten the war.

Lincoln was often at odds with leaders of the stodgy

---

30. *Collected Works*, 4:438, 6:410.
31. Lincoln to Vice President Hannibal Hamlin, September 28, 1862, in ibid., 5:444.

bureaucracy of the federal Bureau of Ordnance. He ignored their resistance to funding an experimental "cheese box on a raft"—built in Greenpoint, Brooklyn. The result did nothing less than change history. The USS *Monitor* not only revolutionized the navy, it single-handedly turned back the most devastating attack on the federal navy prior to Pearl Harbor: the rampage of the Confederate iron ship CSS *Virginia* in March 1862. The *Monitor* likely prevented the *Virginia* from steaming toward Washington and thereby officially ushered in the Iron Age at sea. Within months, the Union had launched a virtual armada of ironclads, each featuring a characteristic revolving gun turret—a technology still used on modern American warships.

Lincoln's new interest in military inventions was not limited to the naval side of military operations.

One of Lincoln's White House secretaries, William O. Stoddard, recalled that would-be inventors deposited so many firearms at the White House that his office, crowded with rifles, grenades, and swords, began to look "like a gun shop." Stoddard believed that "every proposed vendor . . . was possessed by the idea that he might make a sale" of new weaponry if "he could induce the President to overrule the decisions of the Bureau of Ordnance." By then, Lincoln's reputation for embracing new military technology had become well-known.[32]

When an old friend from Springfield wrote to propose "a new and secret art of making Gun Powder," Lincoln

---

32. Stoddard quoted in Harold Holzer, ed., *Dear Mr. Lincoln: Letters to the President* (New York: Addison-Wesley, 1993), 174.

replied with a series of chilling questions that made clear that his main concern was how practical and devastating the proposed chemical would be:

Will it explode with as little or less pressure than ordinary gunpowder?

Will it ignite under 300° Celsius?

Will it ignite by a spark, or percussion-cap, like common gunpowder?[33]

During the war, Lincoln ventured to my home state of New York only once on a secret visit that brought him face-to-face with modern military technology. Near West Point, at the Cold Spring foundry, he watched as huge rifled cannons were forged in a vast and fiery furnace, then looked on as the finished products hurled shells across the Hudson River toward the hills lining the opposite shore. He left the region exhilarated by this demonstration of military technology.[34]

Lincoln's fascination with such improvements should not be taken merely as the obsessive compulsion of a frustrated inventor. Pulitzer Prize–winning historian Robert V. Bruce compared Lincoln's gunpowder project to FDR's Oak Ridge Project, though he insisted that in the end, "scientific technology has little effect on war." As Bruce puts it, the

---

33. *Collected Works*, 6:560.
34. Robert V. Bruce, *Lincoln and the Tools of War* (Indianapolis: Bobbs-Merrill, 1956), 187–88.

most important result of innovations in Civil War weapons rested "in their portent, not their performance."[35]

But such postmortem assessments ignore the fact that the Civil War's WMDs took human life on a larger scale than history had ever witnessed. Vastly improved artillery, torpedoes, mines, armored ships, breech-loading guns, and other modern weaponry increased battlefield deaths and exacted a higher toll on the injured who survived. Such was the tolerance for ever-more-deadly technology that in 1864 General Ulysses S. Grant approved a plan to dig a five-hundred-foot mineshaft toward entrenched Confederate troops in Petersburg, Virginia, so that four tons of gunpowder could be detonated underneath them. The explosion created a gaping crater, but the resulting man-to-man fighting proved a disaster, not a triumph, for the Union.

Technology was by no means a godsend in the Civil War. Nor has it been since then. How right Lincoln was about the dangerous seductions of war! Some eighty years later, in the name of democracy, self-defense, and honor, the United States invented the atom bomb and caused a terrible loss of humanity in Japan. Ever since then we have been struggling to put the genie back in the bottle.

However avid Lincoln's desire to swiftly win the war by using the most devastating weapons and tactics, it remained true that his basic position mirrored the traditional "just war" doctrine that offers a number of familiar considerations for determining the justification for resorting to war:

---

35. Robert V. Bruce, *The Launching of Modern American Science, 1846–1876* (New York: Alfred A. Knopf, 1987), 311–12.

Is it a last resort after all reasonable means have been exhausted? Is there a reasonable prospect of success? Is use of force proportional to the situation at hand, the stakes involved, and the danger posed? Is a successful conclusion reasonably foreseeable? Do the means distinguish sufficiently between combatants and noncombatants?

By these standards, the South appears to have had little justification for firing the shots that started the Civil War on April 12, 1861.

After he was elected president, Lincoln repeatedly confided his disinclination to go to war unless he was left with no alternative. Nonetheless, Southern states quickly began seceding from the Union and threatened to occupy federal garrisons. Frustrated by an interregnum of four months between his election and inauguration and restrained by his natural reluctance to express his thoughts before assuming office, Lincoln could do little but sit and wait as the crisis gained momentum.

In his inaugural address on March 4, 1861, Lincoln felt the need to calm the roiling waters and keep the country from breaking apart. The Union, he argued, could be saved without war, but it was worth saving even if war was the inevitable price. In the draft manuscript that he prepared, he pleaded: "Will you hazard so desperate a step, while there is any possibility that any portion of the ills you fly from have no real existence? . . . Will you risk the commission of so fearful a mistake?" And then came another question—almost a dare: "With you, and not with me, is the solemn question of 'Shall it be peace, or a sword.'" With those words hanging in the air, Lincoln planned to conclude his first inaugural address.[36]

In its final form, the language of the inaugural address proved a bit different, but the general message was unchanged. Lincoln implored his fellow countrymen to "think calmly, and well," before choosing conflict. "Nothing valuable," he pointed out, " can be lost by taking time." The possibility of stepping back from the brink of conflict was crucial to the incoming president. "You can have no conflict," he reminded his Southern adversaries, "without being yourselves the aggressors . . . There needs to be no bloodshed or violence." Putting it another way, he argued: "If there be an object to hurry any of you, in hot haste, to a step which you would never take deliberately, that object will be frustrated by taking time; but no good object can be frustrated by it." Generations later, the tug between good intentions and "hot haste" would continue to animate arguments over war and peace.

In a way, Lincoln's warnings, unheeded in their own time, are as valuable today as they were then. "Passion" and "haste" could destroy "affection" and "the better angels of our nature," he had said.[37] And unchecked, they would rule—and ruin.

When finally, despite all his importuning and manipulation, the war was made inevitable by the South, Lincoln chose to put down the rebellion without the consent of Congress, which was out of session when Southern guns fired on Fort Sumter in 1861. The federal garrison formally surrendered on Sunday, April 14. The very next day, Lincoln

---

36. *Collected Works,* 4:255, 261.
37. Ibid., 4:270–71.

issued a proclamation that acknowledged the insurrection, asked for 75,000 militia from the Northern states, and called the House and Senate back to Washington for an extraordinary but symbolic session nearly three months later on Independence Day. In short order, he issued another proclamation to institute a blockade of Confederate ports and called for more volunteers. Then, after taking note of a strong showing of flag-waving political fervor in the North and particularly in New York City, the beleaguered president set about to craft a war message that would seek the legislative support that he had been unable to summon when the hostilities broke out.

In July, months after his initial proclamations, Lincoln called upon Congress to give the government "the legal means for making this contest a short, and a decisive one," the authority to raise 400,000 troops, and the $400 million needed to fund them. It would be an unquestionably expensive war, especially in those years before billions and trillions became commonplace. But, Lincoln convincingly argued, "A right result, at this time, will be worth more to the world, than ten times the men, and ten times the money."[38]

No war, Lincoln reasoned, could be more just; and all wars, he knew from experience, needed just cause and popular support to pursue. Lincoln called for a "people's contest," summoning "the patriotic instinct of the plain people" who he believed "understand, without an argument, that destroying the government, which was made by Washington, means no good to them." In America there could be no appeal from the ballot to the bullet, he reminded Congress.

---

38. *Collected Works*, 4:431–32.

"Such will be a great lesson of all kingly oppressions" once the American experiment had endured.[39]

Not surprisingly, Lincoln's disinclination to go to war unless absolutely unavoidable made the notion of preemptory war abhorrent. He had said so years earlier in a justly famous letter to his friend William Herndon:

> Allow the President to invade a neighboring nation, whenever *he* shall deem it necessary to repel an invasion, and you allow him to do so, *whenever he may choose to say* he deems it necessary for such purpose—and you allow him to make war at pleasure. Study to see if you can fix *any limit* to his power in this respect, after you have given him so much as you propose. If, to-day, he should choose to say he thinks it necessary to invade Canada, to prevent the British from invading us, how could you stop him? You may say to him, "I see no probability of the British invading us" but he will say to you "be silent; I see it, if you dont."[40]

Lincoln was not denying that self-defense is always justifiable. It is clear that Lincoln would not have given up the right to strike first if there had been a viable capacity on the part of an enemy to strike a lethal blow without notice and a clear intention to do so. In 2002 our president claimed as much concerning Iraq. Jefferson Davis, the Mississippi senator who became the first and only president of the Confederacy, argued: "He who makes the assault is not necessar-

---

39. *Collected Works*, 4:439.
40. Lincoln to Herndon, February 15, 1848, in ibid,, 1:451–52.

ily he who strikes the first blow or fires the first gun. To have awaited further strengthening of their position by land and naval forces, with hostile purpose now declared," he added in justification of the attack on Fort Sumter, "would have been as unwise as it would be to hesitate to strike down the arm of the assailant, who levels a deadly weapon at one's breast, until he has actually fired."[41]

But Lincoln's keen mind, inveterate caution, and strong aversion to violence would have insisted on inarguable proof. In the end, it is fair to say that President Bush settled for much less than that and so did Jefferson Davis.

Lincoln's disinclination to start a killing war would also have argued against the imprudent early relaxation of the military effort to break up al-Qaeda in Afghanistan—and the precipitant involvement in Iraq—without an intelligent plan or the resources to handle the tremendous burden of reconstruction that was made inevitable by our attack. Lincoln knew that once commenced, war must be prosecuted—not with "elder-stalk squirts, charged with rose water"—as he sarcastically told a Louisiana loyalist in 1862. He would not "deal lighter blows rather than heavier ones." He would not "give up the contest, leaving any available means unapplied."[42]

Nor would he stretch American military strength too thin abroad, even if such incursions might increase his popularity at home. When in April 1861, during the *Trent* affair, Secretary of State William H. Seward advised Lincoln that

---

41. Richard N. Current, *Lincoln and the First Shot* (New York: J. B. Lippincott, 1963), 183.
42. Lincoln to Cuthbert Bullitt, July 28, 1862, in *Collected Works*, 5:346.

war with Great Britain might be inevitable and might have a positive effect by uniting the country against a common foreign enemy, Lincoln wisely resisted. "There will be no war," he told Senator Charles Sumner at the height of the crisis with England that December, "unless England is bent upon having one." For Lincoln, it would be "one war at a time."[43]

Similarly, when Napoleon III dispatched armed forces to Mexico to prop up his handpicked "emperor" Maximilian, Lincoln refused to be drawn into an expanded conflict there—especially in the country where Lincoln had seen an unjustifiable war pursued by an earlier president. War with France was to be avoided, not pursued. "Napoleon has taken advantage of our weakness in our time of trouble," the president admitted to General John M. Thayer. Nevertheless, he cautioned, "my policy is, attend to only one trouble at a time." Even when those troubles eased and the Union seemed headed for victory, Lincoln ignored recommendations from his own political allies that he use his enormous armies to march into Canada and annex it. No such ambitions, he insisted, could excuse further bloodshed.[44]

Perhaps President Bush was finally mindful of Lincoln's lesson of one war at a time when he decided to take a markedly less bellicose position with North Korea and Iran than he had hinted at when he called them—along with Iraq—an "axis of evil."

From all this evidence, it is surely reasonable to conclude that had he been available, Lincoln would have urged Presi-

43. David Herbert Donald, *Lincoln* (New York: Simon & Schuster, 1995), 321–22, 413.
44. Don E. and Virginia Fehrenbacher, *Recollected Words of Abraham Lincoln* (Palo Alto, CA: Stanford University Press, 1996), 444.

dent Bush to continue, at least for a while longer, the diplomacy needed to create a coalition with the United Nations to offer Saddam Hussein exile in return for a peaceful turnover of power. President Bush admitted that this would have been a good deal, but he never made the effort it required. Ultimately, he shifted arguments, contending—without proof, as it turned out—that Saddam Hussein had amassed weapons of mass destruction and had conspired with al-Qaeda to use them against both America and his own people.

Lincoln came to the presidency unprepared. His cabinet was an odd assortment of political necessities instead of a group of familiar and trusted advisers who might have helped him make better judgments in his first months. His intelligence concerning what was going on in the South was also meager. The incumbent Democratic president's presence until the end of March 1861 was a problem as well; but Lincoln's proclivity for evasion, still burdening him at this stage in his career, might have been his greatest impediment. The charge has been made—not unreasonably—that these problems caused a failure of diplomacy that destroyed any chance of avoiding war entirely. Maybe so. In any case, Lincoln's experience should have been an instruction to President Bush whose diplomatic skills also were tested in the early days of his presidency and proved wanting. Had George Bush paid closer attention to his hero's early diplomatic difficulties, he might have tried harder to remedy his own.

Perhaps the most significant difference between Lincoln's war and Bush's is not the difference between Bush's eagerness to make war and Lincoln's attempts to avoid it, but rather the nature of the motivations that moved the two leaders to finally engage in fierce hostilities and the results they achieved.

President Lincoln's objective was to preserve the Union for its own sake and the world's because, as he so clearly saw, the idea of a republican democracy represented by the United States had incalculable value to the entire world. Lincoln also seized the opportunity to begin the process of ridding the nation of slavery. Both objectives were achieved, and America's great potential was unleashed. No one seriously disputes the boldness and grandness of these accomplishments.

On the other hand, President Bush's rationales have been vague and, to some extent, contradictory and are still so much in flux that it is difficult to know precisely what is being achieved and at what cost.

President Bush took the nation into a war against terrorism specifically abjuring "nation building." It began in Afghanistan where we knew al-Qaeda, led by Osama bin Laden, was headquartered. They are the admitted perpetrators of 9/11 and the leaders of the terrorist movement aimed at the United States.

After a while, however, our main force was abruptly directed away from this target to a target of greater political opportunity, Saddam Hussein. Although he has since been captured, the effort left hundreds of Americans dead, hundreds more wounded, and cost many thousands of Iraqi lives. It also required that we relax the attacks on al-Qaeda and bin Laden because we were not able to fight two all-out wars at the same time.

Moreover, having captured Hussein and seized Iraq, it is not at all clear how we will help Iraq become a free nation and what precise effect this will have on terrorism, if any.

The plain truth appears to be that even after we have permanently rid the world of the treachery of Saddam Hussein and Osama bin Laden, we will only have removed some of the most visible tumors produced by the cancer of terrorism. Extirpating the tumor leaves the cancer to be dealt with—a cancer perhaps more virulent than ever, lurking in the hovels and hearts of irate terrorists spread around the world, driven to anger by false teachings, financed by money from a number of Arab nations, provoked further by the ongoing struggle in Israel, and threatening a still largely unprotected American homeland.

The Civil War is over: Lincoln, the United States, and the world won.

Bush's war is still mired at "Gettysburg" at a high watermark that may well be followed by years of further bloodshed, with all its pain, all its uncertainty, and with reconstruction still ahead.

Civil Liberties

IT WOULD BE BETTER for Americans if President Bush had been inspired by his avowed mentor Abraham Lincoln to be more cautious, careful, and prepared before beginning his preemptive war in Iraq. And it certainly would be better for us if he had *not* been inspired by Lincoln when it came to the suspension of constitutional rights in the name of security. Faced with the possible disintegration of the Union, Lincoln severely distended—and in some cases violated— the Constitution.

The writ of habeas corpus is one of the fundamental constitutional guarantees of personal liberty, assuring a person detained by the government an opportunity to challenge the detention before a court or judge. There is no question that Lincoln took it upon himself to authorize suspending the writ in contradiction of the Constitution as interpreted by the Supreme Court. He also suppressed two established newspapers, provided unappropriated funds for the purchase of military equipment, allowed a military tribunal to convict Maryland civilian John Merryman without bringing specific charges (to the horror of the still-reigning, eighty-five-year-old Chief Justice Roger B. Taney), and even signed the first income tax act, all in apparent violation of the law.

The facts are these. When Fort Sumter fell, Lincoln determined to go on the offensive to save the Union and democracy. To "surrender the government without a blow" was unacceptable he felt. "There is no Washington in that," he noted with rather uncharacteristic bravado, "—no Jackson in that—no manhood and honor in that."[45]

Two weeks later he ordered his own chief general to ignore the privilege of the writ of habeas corpus "at any point" between Philadelphia and Washington, although he then conceded that even "the bombardment of their cities" was not as extreme as suspending the writ. Lincoln did this to guarantee the safe passage of Union recruits en route to protect the capital and to effectively prevent the Maryland legislature from convening a secession convention.[46] Lincoln feared that the result of such a convention would take Maryland out of the Union and completely isolate Washington. By May the president had also suspended the writ in Florida in order to "remove from the vicinity of United States fortresses all dangerous or suspected persons" during the period of insurrection.[47]

And in 1862, and again in 1863, Lincoln suspended the writ nationwide, unleashing a spate of arbitrary arrests, long imprisonments without formal charges, and military trials of civilians. In one celebrated case, one of the North's most

---

45. Statement to a Baltimore committee, April 22, 1861, in *Collected Works*, 4:341.
46. Ibid., 4:344–47.
47. Ibid., 4:365.

vocal antiwar Democrats, Ohio congressman Clement L. Vallandigham, was arrested by the military and banished to Confederate lines. When the Confederacy refused to accept him, he was sent off to Canada.

To his political opponents in the Union, Lincoln's unprecedented assumption of extraordinary war powers, even in the midst of civil war, revealed him to be a tyrant. The accusation would dog him throughout his presidency and would surface with particular vehemence during the 1864 presidential campaign. But Lincoln always maintained that he had assumed war powers to avoid a "ruinous waste of time," and he believed his actions were "indispensable to the public safety" and were necessary to preserve the Union.[48] He also chose to allow the 1864 election to go forward. "We cannot have free government without free elections," he explained afterward, "and if the rebellion could force us to forgo, or postpone a national election, it might fairly claim to have already conquered and ruined us."[49]

That same day Lincoln admitted: "It has long been a grave question whether any government, not *too* strong for the liberties of its people, can be strong *enough* to maintain its own existence, in great emergencies."[50] Historians—and politicians—have been arguing this point ever since. Lincoln scholar Mark E. Neely, Jr., in his Pulitzer Prize–winning study, *The Fate of Liberty*, asserts that Lincoln meant no usurpation of the Constitution by his actions and sincerely

---

48. From the June 12, 1863, response to a Democratic protest signed by Erastus Corning and others, in *Collected Works*, 6:263.
49. Ibid., 8:101.
50. From a response to an election victory serenade, Washington, D.C., November 10, 1864, in ibid., 8:100.

believed that only by suspending liberty could he preserve it for all time. Others, most recently the author Thomas DiLorenzo, who is often critical of Lincoln, maintain that no goal or good outcome could possibly rationalize Lincoln's ruthless wartime violations of constitutional rights.

Other presidents have behaved similarly in times of war, beginning with John Adams's enthusiastic support for the Alien and Sedition Acts in 1798 to 1800, continuing with the internment of Japanese Americans and Italian Americans during World War II, and now ending with the transgressions of the Bush administration that threaten to set a new record for flagrant disregard of the Constitution.

American citizens have been seized by the executive branch of government and imprisoned without the constitutional protections of the right to counsel and a fair trial. President Bush claims he can order such arrests simply by stating—without having to prove—that the American citizen is an "enemy combatant."

Because of the Patriot Act, now considered improvident even by some of those who voted for it, federal agents now have broad new powers to "sneak and peak" in nonterrorism cases. They may secretly enter a private home without a warrant and keep the fact that they have been there a secret from the owners or occupants for months thereafter.

The Justice Department also has issued regulations authorizing the secret monitoring of attorney-client relationships on presidential authority alone.

Attorney General John Ashcroft began this erosion of constitutional requirements immediately after 9/11 when the Patriot Act was passed by a Republican-dominated Congress and signed by President Bush. This immediately drew vigorous protests from some Americans. The protests were strong enough that, despite continuing terrorist attacks around the world, Republicans in Congress pushed through a repeal of the act's more blatant intrusions on privacy.

In face of strong opposition, President Bush was said to be considering incursions on the Bill of Rights with the proposed Victory Act, short for Vital Interdiction of Criminal Terrorist Organizations Act of 2003. Hundreds of people, including children and at least one American citizen, have been detained for months, charged with no crime and barred from speaking with an attorney. The proposed Victory Act would allow the attorney general to use "administrative subpoenas" to conduct searches and other investigations without the need for judicial approval. Other possibilities being discussed were the right of federal officials to terminate the citizenship of anyone who provides material support to or participates in terrorism. The judgment of guilt would not be made by a court but by appointed bureaucrats in the Department of Justice.

This widespread suspension, and threatened suspension, of constitutionally guaranteed privileges is already being attacked in the courts; and some of the incursions are sure to be turned back by the judiciary once the current heat of war subsides. This is what happened after the Civil War in the *Ex parte Milligan* case. During war and other emergencies the Supreme Court has historically given presidents leeway in using powers not delegated to them specifically—or even powers that contradict the language of the Constitution. After the war or emergency has ended and political pressure has subsided, the Court has then reaffirmed its proper role as guardian of the Constitution. This syndrome has been described by Vice President Al Gore as "a recurring cycle of excess and regret."[51]

Although the courts have always given considerable deference to claims of military necessity, the Supreme Court's willingness, over the strong objection of the Bush administration, to consider appeals involving the detention of so-called enemy combatants based on meager or no proof indicates that even this dominantly conservative Supreme Court may have had enough of Bush's imperial approach to the question of the chief executive's power to override the Constitution. By agreeing to review these cases the court has asserted that it, not the president, continues to have the last word on constitutionality.

When Lincoln was challenged in a similar way, he was, not surprisingly, able to articulate persuasive-sounding defenses. He conceded that he had bent the law severely, if not broken it; but he maintained that had he not done so, the nation would have been lost. No law, he argued, was worth, or should compel, such a result. As he told a group of Albany Democrats in 1863:

> You claim that men may, if they choose, embarrass those whose duty it is, to combat a giant rebellion, and then be dealt with in turn, only as if there was no rebellion. The constitution itself rejects this view. The military arrests and detentions, which have been made . . .

---

51. From his speech on freedom and security delivered on November 9, 2003, in Washington, D.C.

have been for *prevention,* and not for *punishment*—as injunctions to stay injury, as proceedings to keep the peace.[52]

Lincoln had a way of personalizing even the most abstract arguments, a talent that made his explanations both palatable and unforgettable. Defending his broad use of executive authority to the Albany opposition in 1863, he selected a vivid example, asking:

> Must I shoot a simple-minded soldier boy who deserts, while I must not touch a hair of a wiley [*sic*] agitator who induces him to desert? This is none the less injurious when effected by getting a father, or brother, or friend, into a public meeting, and there working upon his feelings, till he is persuaded to write the soldier boy, that he is fighting in a bad cause, for a wicked administration of a contemptable government too weak to arrest and punish him if he shall desert. I think that in such a case, to silence the agitator, and save the boy, is not only constitutional, but, withal, a great mercy.[53]

Of course what Lincoln was saying, as touching as it sounds, might be translated into something like this: If the government thinks a war is a good idea but a citizen thinks it is an abomination and a fraud, he is not free to say so because he might convince someone.

Two jurists I know and respect have differing opinions

52. *Collected Works,* 6:303.
53. Ibid., 266–67.

of Lincoln's actions. Joseph Bellacosa, a jurist and teacher whom I appointed to New York State's Court of Appeals, who is now the dean of St. John's University Law School, has thought the problem through for years and maintains that Lincoln acted above the law. While recognizing that expediency—the national emergency triggered by secession and rebellion—helped to explain Lincoln's actions, Bellacosa nevertheless maintains, "the actions Mr. Lincoln authorized were *ultra vires*, or at least excessive and overboard, geographically and otherwise. They represent the use of raw, unilateral executive power and questionable means to attain some debatable though desirable ends in a concededly horrific set of exigent circumstances that can only be fairly described as lessers among evil choices." Bellacosa proffers what he calls a perhaps unanswerable "hard question"—one certainly worth posing, then and now—"Was the real goal of this extraordinary deprivation of liberties and due process the lofty preservation of the Union—or was the activity a shield for suppressing powerful political opposition and dissenting expression and a sword for enforcing conscription?" And he responds to his own question: "To be sure, mixed motives were at work."[54]

Another jurist whom I respect, Lincoln scholar Frank J. Williams, who contributed to our New York State Lincoln on Democracy Project in 1990 and who has since ascended to the post of chief justice of Rhode Island, disagrees.

---

54. Joseph W. Bellacosa, "Above the Law? Arbitrary Arrests, Habeas Corpus, and Freedom of the Press in Lincoln's New York," in Harold Holzer, ed., *State of the Union: New York and the Civil War* (New York: Fordham University Press, 2002), 68–69.

Lincoln was in a no-win position. He would be condemned, regardless of his actions. If he did not uphold all the provisions of the Constitution, he would be assailed not only by those who genuinely valued civil liberty, but also by enemies and opponents whose motive was criticism itself. Far harsher would have been his denunciation of the whole experiment if the democratic American Union failed, as seemed possible given the circumstances. If such a disaster occurred, what benefit would have been gained by adhering to a fallen Constitution? It was a classic example of the conflict: Do the ends justify the means?[55]

Writing more than a decade ago, the historian Mark E. Neely, Jr., said: "If a situation were to arise again in the United States where the writ of habeas corpus were suspended, government would probably be as ill-prepared to define the legal situation as it was in 1861. The clearest lesson is that there is no clear lesson . . . no neat precedents, no ground rules, no map. War and its effect on civil liberties remain a frightening unknown."[56] Neely was saying in effect that during a war the courts are liable to throw the rule book away. Surely, from time to time they have.

Whatever the validity of Lincoln's judgment under the circumstances he confronted, at least he acknowledged that only in the kind of emergency he faced should a president ignore the Constitution as he did. He also emphatically promised a return to strict compliance with the Constitu-

---

55. Bellacosa, "Above the Law?", 73.
56. Mark E. Neely, Jr., *The Fate of Liberty, Abraham Lincoln and Civil Liberties* (New York: Oxford University Press, 1992), 235.

tion as soon as peace returned. Further mitigation of his conduct may be found in Lincoln's insistence that free elections continue in the North despite the military mobilization, rebellion, and armed conflict that gave him a chance to cancel them. His administration endured huge losses in the off-year congressional elections of 1862, probably in part because Lincoln had further tested his constitutional authority dramatically only six weeks earlier by issuing the Emancipation Proclamation.

Notwithstanding, however, Lincoln's clever attempts at exculpation, or at least mitigation, and his advocates' pleas for understanding the dire circumstances he faced, I still wish that the great Lincoln had stood by the Constitution despite the strong temptation not to. Our government has ample authority under the Constitution to take those steps that are genuinely necessary for our security. At the same time, our system demands that government act only on the basis of measures that have been the subject of open and thoughtful debate in Congress and among the American people and that invasions of the liberty or equal dignity of any individual are subject to review by courts that are open to those affected and independent of the government that is curtailing freedom.

Lincoln's willingness to put himself above the law was particularly unfortunate because of the strong pledge to constitutional fidelity he had made and affirmed in his earlier days. In his Lyceum speech of 1838 he went so far as to say that compliance with the letter and the spirit of the law should be treated as the "political religion" of the nation.[57]

----

57. *Collected Works,* 1:108.

If that were the case, his transgressions during the war were political heresy, a heresy that made it easier for later presidents, including FDR and George W. Bush, to put aside the law for convenience's sake.

Moreover, the example set by Lincoln might have helped influence even Supreme Court justices to believe that there are times when they should put aside their own sworn commitment to the Constitution in order to reach what they believe is an end so vital that it would justify otherwise illicit means. Might that have occurred, for example, in a case in which their one vote was enough to elect to the presidency someone they preferred, someone who would otherwise have been defeated?

I believe the Supreme Court was closer to the truth in *Ex parte Milligan* than in the later cases that ignored its ruling because protecting against the deterioration or dissolution of our Bill of Rights can be the highest form of patriotism, in war as well as peace.

I wish Abraham Lincoln and George W. Bush agreed.

The Role of Government

SOME OF THE MOST rancorous political debates today revolve around the question of what precise role the government should play beyond the most obvious one, which is to protect us from enemies who seek to injure or destroy the nation.

The strong strain of individuality that survived our coming together as one nation in 1776 and maintained itself during the reaffirmation of that Union in 1865 continues to provide sharp differences of opinion. Thus, those who today call themselves conservatives are inclined to disparage government in general and big government in particular. In fact, this position is much more rhetorical than it is real. This appears to be lost on many of us who take sides in the argument because we think people like us—in the same economic, ethnic, religious, or racial group—belong on one side or the other. No one was shocked when President Ronald Reagan made his principal plank one that decried government because he was supported most heavily by people who paid the most for the government through taxes—as opposed to the people who needed government the most.

So those who call themselves conservatives like President Reagan are inclined rhetorically to disparage government. Some of them call government an essential evil to be minimized in every way possible because it tends to discourage private initiative, reward the indolent, and unfairly redistribute wealth from those who succeed and deserve it to those who have failed and not earned it.

Many others argue that government has a crucial role to play in spreading the so-called safety net that protects otherwise helpless Americans from deprivation and destruction and in helping all Americans enhance their productivity. They point to the successful programs invented by Franklin Delano Roosevelt in response to the Great Depression—Social Security, Home Relief for the poor, the WPA—and the subsequent scores of other affirmative government programs established by the Republican and Democratic administrations that followed. Notable among them were Truman's Marshall Plan, Eisenhower's Highway Act, John Kennedy's space program, Lyndon Johnson's Medicare and Medicaid laws, Richard M. Nixon's jobs legislation and environmental protection laws, and Carter's Chrysler bailout.

In all these cases, the political judgment followed a simple criterion—we should have only the government we need but we should also have *all* the government we need if the market won't provide it. Although the Constitution does not require these acts of government, Republican and Democratic presidents alike have decided that the people needed them because private enterprise would not or could not adequately supply them. In fact, these initiatives have since been so well accepted by the American people that the modern American conservative presidents—most recently Reagan and the two Bushes—would be no more inclined to explicitly attack such ingrained programs than they would defense spending and family values—except maybe when speaking privately to other conservatives. Conservatives like our current President Bush have little trouble arguing for huge government programs that go directly to assist large corporate interests, such as exemptions from taxes, excessive purchases of dubious usefulness, farm subsidies for large corporate farmers, and the like. At the same time, they continue their instinctual reluctance to use government to provide help to struggling Americans by seeking to limit basic assistance programs like school lunches, public education, public housing, aid to veterans, Medicaid, and Social Security. Recently they pushed for a $400 billion Medicare program that, in fact, would move toward a shrinkage of government help in favor of private corporate health care.

From our earliest days, this antigovernment impulse has inspired political attempts to prevent government from assuming functions not explicitly required by the Constitution. For example, Alexander Hamilton's proposed national bank ignited furious opposition from James Madison and Thomas Jefferson and later from Andrew Jackson.

Lincoln was able to get to the heart of this matter. Although he was often called a conservative, especially when talking about conserving the principles of the Declaration of Independence, he was distinguished by his unique ability to sublimate political ideology in favor of common sense and pragmatism. In notes that he composed around 1854, he concluded that even in a perfect world—where "all men were just"—"there still would be *some* . . . need of government."[58] And that was before the Civil War required the unprecedented government involvement in everyday life that resulted in the Homestead Act, the Pacific Railway Act, the Morrill Act, the National Banking Act, conscription, a uniform currency, daily mail delivery to homes, and even a federal income tax.

Perhaps Lincoln's most valuable contribution to the argument was providing a cogent plain-English formula for determining what specific functions government should undertake. Around 1854 he honed his credo and described the role of government with sparkling simplicity. He said, "The legitimate object of government is 'to do for the people what needs to be done, but which they can not, by individual effort, do at all, or do so well, for themselves.'"[59]

With the prescience that was another one of his great gifts, Lincoln made clear that the need for government would grow as the world's population grew larger and people's interactions grew more intense when he added:

> But a far larger class of objects springs from the injustice of men. If one people will make war upon another, it is a necessity with that other to unite and cooperate for defense. Hence the military department. If some men will kill, or beat, or constrain others, or despoil them of property, by force, fraud, or noncompliance with contracts, it is a common object with peaceful and just men to prevent it.[60]

---

58. Fragment on government, ca. July 1854, in *Collected Works*, 2:221.
59. From a revised fragment, ibid.
60. Ibid.,2:221.

There is no doubt that Lincoln was unshakably convinced that government intelligently used was not the evil
force described by President Reagan and his followers. History since then has vindicated Lincoln's conviction with a
long series of government innovations that have helped
make America the world's most powerful nation and the
greatest engine of opportunity in the world.

Lincoln was as astute in detecting and correcting government's weaknesses as he was at knowing its strength;
and the greatest of these weaknesses was, of course, slavery,
which had been preserved in the Constitution. He focused
the nation's attention on this government-protected oppression: "We made the experiment; and the fruit is before us.
Look at it—think of it."[61] He spent the rest of his life
using government to end that evil experiment.

Lincoln obviously never had to deal with issues like environmental standards and the minimum wage, let alone
government health care and other social services. But it is
clear that, in a modern incarnation, Lincoln would not accept President Ronald Reagan's famous diagnosis that "the
problem *is* government." Lincoln believed that government
offered possibility, protection, and advancement and, at its
best, would encourage rather than discourage both personal
initiative and contributions to the greater community. His
actions supported his words. In his early days in politics as
a young state legislator in Illinois he came out enthusiastically for "internal improvements"—the nineteenth-century
term for what today we call—more awkwardly—"infrastructure" for economic development. Not everyone shared

---

61. From a revised fragment in *Collected Works*, 2:222.

his enthusiasm for the financing of railroads and canals. Many argued that this kind of financing should be left entirely to private enterprise, but Lincoln's allies prevailed and the law took effect. The result, as it happened, threw the state into debt; but the transportation infrastructure of Illinois was modernized. Despite the unanticipated financial exposure, Lincoln never lost his enthusiasm for government investment in transportation.

He also found it easy to surmount a constitutional objection that was raised against federal investment in local projects. As historian Gabor Boritt has observed, "Lincoln could not see liberty and democracy threatened by such aid—quite the opposite."[62] On the House floor as a freshman Congressman, he continued to advocate for internal improvements, suggesting:

> Let the nation take hold of the larger works, and the states the smaller ones; and thus, working in a meeting direction, discreetly, but steadily and firmly, what is made unequal in one place may be equalized in another, extravagance avoided, and the whole country put on the career of prosperity, which shall correspond with its extent of territory, its natural resources, and the intelligence and enterprize of its people."[63]

Lincoln would likely be shocked if he could see the deterioration plaguing America's railways and highways today because

---

62. Gabor S. Boritt, *Lincoln and the Economics of the American Dream* (Memphis: Memphis State University Press, 1978), 131–32.

63. Speech on internal improvements before the U.S. House of Representatives, June 22, 1848, in *Collected Works,* 1: 488.

recent governments have lacked Lincoln's commitment. Interstate highways built in the 1950s are crumbling in the new millennium. Railroad tracks are so old they cannot accommodate the high-speed trains that routinely carry passengers today in Europe and Asia. Some aging harbors and ports are unable to handle the container ships that carry most of the goods that travel by sea and river; and all airports, shipping ports, and railroads remain frighteningly vulnerable to a proven terrorist capacity to wreak havoc on us. Lincoln would not have failed to understand that only government is capable of supplying the mass access and dependable security our people need.

Faced with secession and rebellion in 1861, Lincoln was obviously thinking about the role of government more than ever. No Northern homes were being threatened; the South asked only to separate from the country unmolested. But Lincoln would not have it; not just because he revered the Union made by the founders, but because he revered its modern manifestation, too—a functioning, active, and helpful government. That year he forcefully reminded Congress that

> the leading object of the government for whose existence we contend" [is] . . . a struggle for maintaining in the world, that form, and substance of government, whose leading object is, to elevate the condition of men—to lift artificial weights from all shoulders—to clear the paths of laudable pursuit for all—to afford all, an unfettered start, and a fair chance, in the race of life.[64]

---

64. Message to Congress, July 4, 1861, in *Collected Works*, 4:438.

So Lincoln reached out for the "penniless beginner" and insisted that every "poor man" should be given his chance and that government should help if private effort wasn't enough. Always at the heart of his struggle and his yearning was the passion to use government to make room for the outsider and the insistence upon a commitment to respect the idea of equality by fighting for inclusion. Diversity, he believed, was not a matter of discord but was one of "the very cements of this Union. They don't make the house a house divided against itself," he added, alluding to his own famous warning: "They are the props that hold up the house."[65]

That is not to suggest that Lincoln was reckless in his willingness to spend money on government. Gabor Boritt makes it clear that even as Lincoln was boldly proposing and supporting new revenue-raising measures in Illinois, he was prudently insisting on various austerity limits on spending.[66] Lincoln made known his great concern about the growth of government during the Civil War, as well. Writing to his Secretary of War in 1864, he acknowledged that "the government has a difficult duty to perform . . . paying for the war while trying to help with other of the peoples' needs."[67] But at the moment the government was most severely challenged, Lincoln preserved the idea of a state that actively fostered inclusion and unity and was willing to spend its resources investing in those objectives, albeit prudently.

In 1864 Lincoln told a regiment of Ohio soldiers that "this government must be preserved in spite of the acts of any

---

65. *Collected Works*, 3:478, 121.
66. Boritt, *Lincoln and the Economics of the American Dream*, 42–48.
67. Lincoln to Edwin M. Stanton, March 18, 1864, in *Collected Works*, 7:255.

man or set of men." But his call to action was not abstract. The government was worth saving because it was not merely an idea but also an instrument. "It is worthy of your every effort," he told the soldiers, because "nowhere in the world is presented a government of so much liberty and equality. To the highest and poorest amongst us are held out the highest privileges and positions. The present moment finds me at the White House, yet there is as good a chance for your children as there was for my father's." To Lincoln, such was the essential promise of government of, by, and for the people.

As he pointed out that day, "We are striving to maintain the government and institutions of our fathers, to enjoy them ourselves, and transmit them to our children and our children's children forever."[68]

Franklin Delano Roosevelt defended his numerous nation-serving governmental programs by citing Lincoln in his second fireside chat in 1934:

> The course we have followed fits the American practice of courageous recognition of change. I believe with Abraham Lincoln, that "The legitimate object of government, is to do for a community of people, what they need to have done, but can not do, at all, or can not, so well do, for themselves—in their separate and individual capacities."[69]

Beginning with President Ronald Reagan in 1981, modern conservative Republican rhetoric has attempted to turn

---

68. August 31, 1864, in *Collected Works*, 7:528.

69. Mark E. Neely, Jr., "FDR and Lincoln: A Democratic President Shapes the Story of a Republican President's Life," *Lincoln Lore* (June 1975).

the nation back toward a dog-eat-dog fight for survival where the littlest dogs are left to only the resources and mercy of their family and whatever charities might be available. Conservative spokespeople like former Speaker Newt Gingrich and Congressman Tom DeLay of Texas have been unabashed in their desire to replace as many government programs as possible with the market system that preceded the programs. Those conservative desires have not been quashed, but the need for government to provide what a faltering economy has failed to provide is too obvious and too urgent to be politically ignored. President Bush would be hard pressed to argue today that government is the problem, when his federal government is spending more freely than most governments in modern history, including providing hundreds of millions of dollars that even some Republicans call "corporate welfare."

After the Republicans boasted of having produced more than $2 trillion in tax cuts, the federal budget recorded a huge new deficit, the largest in our history. Despite this shortfall, President Bush then told America that we desperately needed to have government spend $87 billion more to shore up the troubled effort to reconstruct Iraq and help establish its first democratically selected government—all part of the president's optional war.

A close reading of the nation's political history since 1980 makes clear that while the two Bush presidencies were distinctly more discreet than Reagan's about admitting their strong dislike for government, they nevertheless sought to achieve a shrinking of programs designed to avoid the pain and lost opportunities created by privatization and "starving the beast." This brutally revealing metaphor for government was one of the political motives for the Reagan administration's huge tax cuts that went mostly to the wealthiest Americans. In part, the intent of the cuts was to deplete vital resources for the government programs created and nurtured by more than half a century of administrations, Democratic and Republican alike.

President George H. Bush started his presidency with a pledge of "Read my lips, no new taxes." But then, saddled by the huge deficits created by his predecessor's attempts to starve the beast, he was forced to break his pledge and raise taxes. President Clinton, who had a much less jaundiced view of government, followed Bush with another tax increase limited to those most capable of paying it. A few years after the two tax increases the government—and its people—had the benefit of the greatest four years of prosperity in American history, including 22 million new jobs and the largest budget surplus ever. That is the kind of peace and prosperity the nation dreams of, but today's reality has crushed this dream at least for the time being. If halcyon days are to return, it seems clear we will need more government help to bring them back. As Lincoln pointed out,

> This government is expressly charged with the duty of providing for the general welfare . . . I do not mean to say that this general government is charged with the duty of redressing or preventing all the wrongs in the world; but I do think that it is charged with the duty of preventing and redressing all wrongs which are wrongs to itself.[70]

---

70. Speech at Dayton, Ohio, September 17, 1859, in *Collected Works*, 3:460.

IT'S HARD TO believe when President Bush looks at the picture of Abraham Lincoln on his wall in the White House that he feels reassured that he's done what Lincoln would have done in his place either with respect to the budget or with his failure to achieve a stronger coalition with foreign governments at a time when not only the nation but the world can use all the good government it can get. That having been said, let's take a closer look at Lincoln's views concerning the economy, its impact on the American people, and the nation's relationship with the rest of the world.

Opportunity

THREE THINGS ARE MOST obvious about today's American economy: It is astonishingly less successful than the economy produced by the Clinton administration; it is an economy that widens the already large gap between the lucky and the left out by providing more profits to businesses while creating less opportunity for American workers; and it is saddled with tremendous new federal debt and annual deficits that will leave the next generation of Americans paying a frighteningly high price for the excesses and omissions of our current government.

There are obviously huge differences between the economy today and the economy in the last half of the nineteenth century when Lincoln was president. The population of the nation, the size of the world market, the dramatic changes in mobility and communication, the demands of technology, and the aspirations and expectations of the people are all larger, more formidable, more complicated, and more difficult to manage. On the other hand, government in both eras played a role as a facilitator of commerce. In that regard Lincoln can be thought of as an activist president. He fought for internal improvements like railroads and canals from his early days as a Whig in the Illinois legislature, advocating investments by both the federal and state governments. He also took a special interest in national banking, which Alexander Hamilton had introduced as an indispensable governmental function if commerce were to succeed in the new nation. When Hamilton's federal bank disappeared under Andrew Jackson, Lincoln argued for an Illinois bank as an alternative; and when the Illinois banking system collapsed, Lincoln vigorously promoted direct financing from the federal government to the private economy and argued for public education as well.

Today's Republicans and conservatives prefer not to make a point of it, but Lincoln also strongly advocated the raising of taxes at both the state and federal levels as part of his confidence in government's ability to help provide what was needed to give the people of the nation a real opportunity to succeed in our market-system economy.

Until the late 1830s counties taxed land and states taxed nonresidents. At first Lincoln took the position that physical improvements in the state would pay for themselves through bonds and would not require taxes. For education, Lincoln proposed borrowing instead of taxation, but eventually taxation became inevitable for education as well.

Lincoln understood that taxes were despised by most citizens, but he also realized they were necessary and that they had to be made just. To do that, Lincoln promoted systems of progressive taxation that distributed help and assigned burdens on the basis of need and capacity. In 1862 he imposed the first income tax in American history, which was later found to be unconstitutional until the concept of an income tax was embedded in the Constitution by the Thirteenth Amendment. Referring to a local tax he favored, he said, "It does not increase the tax upon the '*many poor*' but upon the '*wealthy few*' by taxing the land that is worth $50 or $100 per acre, in proportion to its value, instead of, as heretofore, no more than that which was worth but $5 per acre. This valuable land, as is well known, belongs, not to the poor, but to the wealthy citizen."[71]

Lincoln tried to raise taxes several times in Congress, championing taxation for improvements and, as Gabor Boritt puts it, he began "to transcend the limitations of American traditions."[72] Lincoln believed that while the power to tax was the power to destroy, it was also the power to keep opportunity alive when used productively So he used it—as Oliver Wendell Holmes said—as "the price we pay for civilization."

Earlier in his career Lincoln supported property taxes— not at a flat rate but at graduated rates that would impose the highest burdens on the owners of the richest lands and homes. Ever the politician, Lincoln sensed that it was not only fair for the wealthy few to pay the most, but good politics, too, since the wealthy few were "not sufficiently numerous to carry elections."[73]

Although several of the individual states—principally in the South—imposed income taxes of their own by the 1850s, the federal government before the Civil War depended on import levies—protective tariffs—for more than 90 percent of its revenues. Lincoln was a high-tariff man from the

---

71. Lincoln to William S. Wait, March 2, 1839, in *Collected Works*, 1:148.

72. Boritt, *Lincoln and the Economics of the American Dream*, 50.

73. *Collected Works*, 1:148, see also Donald, *Lincoln*. 76.

beginning of his career, supporting tariffs not only for their ability to generate funds but also for the help they gave to American industry. By the time he became president, it is fair to say that Lincoln's passion for tariffs had receded and his principal social and economic issue had become slavery.

War revived Lincoln's interest in federal revenues out of necessity. The war proved costly beyond imagining; import duties, the sale of bonds, and bank loans would not begin to cover governmental expenditures. For a year, at the urgent request of the administration, Congress debated a tax bill and finally, in 1862, enacted one that quickly got Lincoln's approval. At long last, the *New York Herald* editorialized, "millionaires" would be required to "contribute a fair proportion of their wealth to the support of the national government."[74]

The revolutionary nature of Lincoln's tax measure cannot be overestimated. It gave the federal government the power to collect levies on tobacco, liquor, photographs, even ferryboat rides, and, most importantly of all, the government imposed a fair, graduated income tax: 3 percent on incomes from $600 to $10,000 and 5 percent on incomes above $10,000. As with so many other examples of daring leadership, Lincoln effectively set a precedent that would rescue—and come to characterize—America.[75]

Nothing is clearer than Lincoln's tenacious belief in the equality of opportunity as declared and implied in the Dec-

---

74. Quoted in Steven R. Weisman, *The Great Tax Wars: Lincoln to Wilson—The Fierce Battles over Money and Power that Transformed the Nation* (New York: Simon & Schuster, 2002), 34.

75. Ibid., 41.

laration of Independence. What can we then fairly speculate that he might say about government economic and fiscal policies that, instead of making badly needed investments in enhancing productivity through education and teaching, give a trillion dollars in tax cuts to wealthy Americans? That's what the supply-side tax cut theory of the Reagan administration did. David Stockman, Reagan's budget guru, admitted candidly that a major purpose of the huge tax cuts was to shrink the discretionary parts of the budget that provided education, health care, and other benefits to the undereducated and neglected. The current administration has followed suit, and the gap between the fortunate few and the Americans who are struggling has grown wider and wider. Executive salaries are now more than five hundred times those of workers; a company's top earners received only ten or eleven times as much as its other workers not that long ago. The wealth at the top of the economic ladder has grown enormously while the middle of the ladder has sagged farther and farther behind. The Republican analyst and commentator Kevin Phillips describes this condition in a powerful and heavily documented work titled *Wealth and Democracy*.[76] Only one of four or five workers is currently highly skilled in America. A few years ago we had to import hundreds of foreign skilled workers to meet our needs. More recently we have begun to export work to skilled workers in India and other countries. Forty-two million Americans who are not poor enough for Medicaid, old enough for Medicare, or lucky enough to have employer-provided health care go

---

76. Kevin Phillips, *Wealth and Democracy: A Political History of the American Rich* (New York: Broadway Books, 2002).

without any health insurance because the cost of health care goes up more than 10 percent a year.

Given current conditions, it is difficult not to believe that Lincoln would have rejected President Bush's supply-side tax cuts since they went to the already rich. Nor is it conceivable that he would have approved of the proposed abolition of all estate taxes.

The estate-tax repeal is a particularly good example of the difference between today's conservatives and Abraham Lincoln with respect to how the burden of taxation should be apportioned. One of the conservative proponents' arguments in favor of repeal is that it is unfair to deny a wealthy person's progeny, or any other heirs, the fruit of that successful individual's labors and enterprise. The estate tax in recent years produced some $30 billion a year and affected only the wealthiest 2 percent of Americans. Poverty, on the other hand, affects one of every six American children. In 1997 almost half the estate tax was paid by less than 2,400 estates. The loss of revenues with the abolition of the estate tax for the deficit-ridden federal budget is projected to be $750 billion a year, several years from now. Estate-tax repeal would further burden state treasuries with a "pick-up" tax, the benefit of which would be lost to the states. The amount of loss as a result of this change is projected to be another $9 billion a year. Charitable giving, encouraged in part by the exemption that estate-tax law provided, would also be diminished.

William H. Gates, Sr., Warren Buffett, and seven hundred other Americans who are among the wealthiest people in the nation have selflessly argued against the repeal, pointing out that their wealth is attributable as much to the many advantages and benefits received from the nation as it is to their own efforts. Therefore, they feel it would be unfair to impose the burden of higher taxes and reduced education, health care, and other social programs on the poor and struggling middle class—a burden that would inevitably result from the repeal of the estate tax. In testimony given to a Senate subcommittee considering the issue, Mr. Gates, president of Responsible Wealth, argued, "A good life should be anything which is achieved. It should not be delivered as a result of the womb you happened to start from." He sounds a great deal like Lincoln.

Lincoln expressed similar thoughts many times. He probably would never have allowed the current scheduled repeal to become law; and if his veto had been overridden, he would be working to change the law before it became effective.

Lincoln insisted that the economy provide every American with what Gabor Boritt calls the "Right to Rise," the opportunity to earn security and a reasonable degree of comfort. And Lincoln believed government should do what was required to ensure that opportunity. In Lincoln's years the "Right to Rise" was still a distant hope.

In January 1860, the year Lincoln sought and won the presidency, many Americans were horrified to read about a terrible tragedy. The Pemberton Mill in Lawrence, Massachusetts, collapsed without warning, killing hundreds of workers, many of whom were young women. During the frantic effort to rescue the survivors, a fire suddenly swept through the ruins, killing many of those who were still alive. The Pemberton Mill tragedy became a rallying point for reformers committed to improving conditions in the American workplace.

Around the same time, some 20,000 shoe workers in Massachusetts began a prolonged and contentious strike for better wages. Strikes were not commonplace in Lincoln's time, but more than twenty New England towns and cities witnessed angry labor rallies in 1859 and 1860. The shoe-industry action ignited a national political controversy, with critics assailing the strike and blaming the workers for crippling the New England economy.

En route to visit his son's private school in New Hampshire, Lincoln paused between trains one day to make a stop at the Pemberton Mill site, which had become something of a tourist attraction. A few days later he made a major speech in New Haven in which he expressed strong support for the striking shoe workers. "I *like* the system which lets a man quit when he wants to," he declared that day, "and wish it might prevail everywhere."[77] Of course he was principally comparing the rights enjoyed by free white workers in the North to the involuntary servitude imposed on millions of blacks in the South, but there was an even larger message on his mind. To Lincoln, the "Right to Rise" was an inseparable part of the American commitment to democracy. He never gave fuller attention to the subject than he did during his long New Haven address:

> I don't believe in a law to prevent a man from getting rich; it would do more harm than good. So while we do not propose any war upon capital, we do wish to allow the humblest man an equal chance to get rich with everybody else. When one starts poor, as most do in the

race of life, free society is such that he knows he can better his condition; he knows that there is no fixed condition of labor, for his whole life. I am not ashamed to confess that twenty-five years ago I was a hired laborer, nailing rails, at work on a flat-boat—just what might happen to any poor man's son! I want every man to have the chance—and I believe a black man is entitled to it—in which he *can* better his condition—when he may look forward and hope to be a hired laborer this year and the next, work for himself afterward, and finally to hire men to work for him! That is the true system.[78]

Lincoln believed it was the responsibility of America's leaders to encourage and (when possible) to facilitate opportunity not to hinder it, whether through perpetuation of slavery or constraining free workers from going out on strike. Lincoln, who rose in life as an attorney representing railroad interests in Illinois, saw no dissonance between the encouragement of profitable industry and the encouragement of an upwardly mobile working class. As his law partner William Herndon later attested, when Southerner George Fitzhugh issued a book condemning unions and strikes, it "aroused the ire of Lincoln more than most proslavery books."[79]

Lincoln not only advocated the American dream; he lived it. No president ever began life in more abject poverty or with less likelihood of success, much less world fame. His father was a wandering farmer who barely made ends meet

---

78. From the speech delivered on March 6, 1860, in *Collected Works*, 4:24–25.
79. Boritt, *Lincoln and the Economics of the American Dream*, 182.

for his family. Young Abraham was compelled to perform manual labor from childhood, planting seeds and clearing woods for fields. When Lincoln was old enough, his father sent him out to work for neighbors and the boy became especially skilled at chopping wood and making rails for fencing. Abe barely enjoyed a year of formal schooling altogether, and until he decided on a career in law—which he basically taught himself from books without attending law school or reading in an attorney's office—he seriously thought about becoming a blacksmith. For the rest of his life he admired and sought to encourage the "penniless beginner" who, like he, dreamed and labored for advancement. He believed in the ability of the poor to improve their lives by succeeding and employing others, thereby creating opportunity for new generations of workers laboring along the same path to success. Lincoln believed in a free society that rewarded hard work with the chance for self-improvement and a government that offered help in achieving this.

During the Civil War, Lincoln would frequently make appearances on the White House grounds to greet regiments marching off to or back from the fighting, to thank them for their valorous service. The words he often used to encourage them reminded the soldiers about their birthright: American opportunity. "I beg you to remember this," he implored one regiment from Ohio, "not merely for my sake, but for yours. I happen temporarily to occupy this big White House. I am a living witness that any one of your children may look to come here as my father's child has." As Lincoln put it that day, the war—and the government it was intended to preserve—was a battle to guarantee for the future "an open field and a fair chance for your industry, enterprise and intelligence; that you may all have equal privileges in the race of life, with all its desirable human aspirations."[80]

Lincoln believed that labor was the creator of all value, while capital was the "fruit of labor." Workingmen, he believed, were the basis of all governments, if for no other reason than that "there are more of them than of any other class," as he put it on his own fifty-second birthday. He favored a capitalist system that put more people to work at better pay and in better conditions. "Free labor," he said, "has the inspiration of hope."[81]

Early in his political career Lincoln spoke on the responsibility of government to facilitate opportunity. "To [give] to each labourer the whole product of his labour, or as nearly as possible, is a most worthy object of any good government." Lincoln never lost sight of the fact that the rebellion was at its core "a war upon the rights of all working people." As he helped to free workers from bondage, he anticipated they would have more than just freedom; he also expected they would enjoy, realistically, the right to rise up the economic ladder. To help them do that he signed bills for homesteaders ("so that every man should have the means and opportunity of benefiting his condition") and laws that established the first land-grant colleges—the precursors of today's vast, still-affordable state university systems.[82]

---

80. August 22, 1864, in *Collected Works*, 7:512.

81. Ibid., 7:259, 4:203; 5:52; 3:462; Boritt, *Lincoln and the Economics of the American Dream*, 176.

82. *Collected Works*, 1:412; 4:203.

Lincoln might be surprised to discover that labor in the United States is weaker today than it was fifty years ago. He surely would be disappointed to learn that, because of the increasing cost of health care, companies are reducing benefits, hiking employee contribution rates, or denying health care entirely. More than 43 million Americans, most of them workers, are already without health insurance. With the median annual household income hovering around $42,000 and growing at only about 1 percent a year and with the cost of health care, education, housing, and transportation growing far more rapidly, most workers are sliding farther and farther down the mountain. Meanwhile we have more millionaires and billionaires than ever, and the gap grows wider between rich and poor with no real hope for a reversal.

Certainly the policies of the second Bush administration offer labor little comfort. The administration opposes benefits for workers whenever possible, trying even to deny workers in the new Homeland Security Department their right to organize. At the same time, it has redistributed much of the nation's wealth to the wealthiest Americans instead of investing it in the education, training, and health care that would enhance the productivity of America's workers.

In late 2003 the Bush administration began touting the economic recovery by pointing out that business profits were up, the stock market was climbing, and output productivity was rising. What they failed to note was that the so-called recovery did little, if anything, for the vast majority of Americans who happen to be workers and not CEOs, large shareholders, or investment bankers. Employment was still more than 2 million jobs less than the year before. New jobs were going to workers overseas while American workers' wages were barely growing at all. The economy was getting stronger, but most Americans weren't realizing the benefits.

The American economy is nearly 70 percent consumption. One of the most serious problems we face today is the inability of the 140 million American workers and their families to buy what they need and what they reasonably desire. In all likelihood, if Lincoln had been here to try stimulating the economy by giving tax cuts to increase the purchase of goods and services, he would have given them to the workers who would be more likely to spend the money than to investors who have all the spending capacity they need.

Lincoln believed that people should work and work hard—"Work, work, work, is the main thing," he told an aspiring lawyer. He had faith that with hard work people would succeed if they were capable. Even in a wartime economy he never abandoned the principle that labor comes before capital in the hierarchy of economic value and that workers should not be trapped in a "fatally fixed condition" for life.[83]

Speaking at an agricultural fair in Milwaukee a little more than a year before he won the presidency, Lincoln set out his vision of the relation between labor and capital:

> The prudent, penniless beginner in the world, labors for wages awhile, saves a surplus with which to buy tools or land, for himself; then labors on his own account another while, and at length hires another new beginner to help him. This, say its advocates, is *free* labor—the just and generous, and prosperous system, which opens the

---

83. Lincoln to John M. Brockman, September 25, 1860, in *Collected Works*, 4:121.

way for all—gives hope to all, and energy, and progress, and improvement of condition to all.[84]

Two years later, in his first annual message to Congress—the nineteenth-century equivalent of today's State of the Union address—Lincoln had changed barely a word in the core philosophy he had enunciated in Milwaukee and New Haven, even after the nation broke in half over the issue of slavery. But echoing his pre-presidential credo, he was prepared to further amplify the doctrine. Now he was willing to liken opportunity to liberty, to state officially what he had been suggesting privately—that the latter was not possible without the former:

> The prudent, penniless beginner in the world, labors for wages awhile, saves a surplus with which to buy tools for himself; then labors on his own account another while, and at length hires another new beginner to help him. This is the just, and generous, and prosperous system, which opens the way to all—gives hope to all, and consequent energy, and progress, and improvement of condition to all. No men living are more worthy to be trusted than those who toil up from poverty—none less inclined to take, or touch, aught which they have not honestly earned. Let them beware of surrendering a political power which they already possess, and which, if surrendered, will surely be used to close the door of advancement against such as they, and to fix new dis-

---

84. September 30, 1859, in *Collected Works*, 3:477–79.

abilities and burdens upon them, till all of liberty shall be lost.[85]

Americans today have too quickly surrendered "a political power which they already possess" and are in danger of seeing the door slammed shut on advancement—and, as Lincoln warned, on liberty itself.

Lincoln reminded Civil War soldiers that they were fighting to preserve their right to rise one day to enjoy as much success as he had—perhaps to achieve the presidency itself. We will have to do much more than we have so far to ensure that the veterans of the wars in Afghanistan and Iraq have the same right when they return home to the country they have defended. We need to provide jobs, health care, and education—a postwar program to encourage opportunity at least as innovative and effective as Lincoln's land grants or FDR's GI Bill.

Every day it is more obvious that the best way to defend our workers against losing their jobs to foreigners is not to banish or severely limit the freedom of trade; it is to better educate and train our workers in the skills required by this new technological age. So far this administration has done little to provide what it will take to raise the number of skilled workers in this country. That is a failure Lincoln probably would not have tolerated.

"I think it is time for us Democrats to claim Lincoln as one of our own," Franklin D. Roosevelt declared as governor

---

85. From Lincoln's first annual message to Congress, December 3, 1861, in *Collected Works*, 5:52–53.

of New York in 1929. "The Republican Party has certainly repudiated, first and last, everything he stood for." Or so it seemed to that future president facing the first devastation of the Great Depression.[86]

Today we do not need to play the label game with Abraham Lincoln—all we have to do is remember what he had hoped the American future would hold for those willing to work to improve their lives.

Lincoln taught us a priceless lesson about the sanctity of American opportunity. No American—leader or voter—should forget the credo he expressed on the eve of his presidency: "I hold the value of life is to improve one's condition. Whatever is calculated to advance the condition of the honest, struggling laboring man, so far as my judgment will enable me to judge of a correct thing, I am for that thing."

America must be for that thing again.

No one knew better than Lincoln that our past is prologue. He loved history and revered America's founders. But as he put it: "While we reverence their memory, let us not forget how vastly greater is our opportunity."[87]

---

86. Neely, "FDR and Lincoln."
87. Letter to Joseph H. Choate, December 19, 1864, in *Collected Works*, 8:170.

Global Interdependence

WHAT PEOPLE NEED from their leaders most of all is a vision of the future that is large, inspiring, clear, and achievable. Great American leaders like Washington, the Roosevelts, John Kennedy, and Martin Luther King, Jr., all had that in common, but it is difficult to dispute the conclusion of the author Donald T. Phillips that "Abraham Lincoln... preached a vision of America that has never been equaled."[88] In his July 4, 1861, message to Congress, Lincoln described his vision this way:

> This is essentially a People's contest. . . . And this issue embraces more than the fate of these United States. It presents to the whole family of man, the question, whether a constitutional republic, or a democracy—a government of the people, by the same people—can, or cannot, maintain its territorial integrity, against its own domestic foes.[89]

---

88. Donald T. Phillips, *Lincoln on Leadership: Executive Strategies for Tough Times* (New York: Warner Books, 1992), 163–65.
89. *Collected Works*, 4:438, 426.

No doubt Lincoln's remarks were directed immediately to the people of the United States, but they also reveal the marvelous scope of his vision, which went far beyond the limits of his own land to encompass the rest of the world— no part of which he had ever seen, but all of which Lincoln consciously included in the basic principles that made him the great leader he was.

To Lincoln, the writers of the Declaration of Independence had made clear that the statements of faith and purpose they had composed applied to all men everywhere because their source was not just the mind and will of a group of heroic rebels in America but also the "Laws of Nature and Nature's God."

As the historian Ralph G. Newman put it, "Only out of his complete assumption of that tenet could have come the determination and staying power to educate himself and literally pull himself up by his own bootstraps . . . he saw the Civil War as the final testing of that almighty principle."[90]

Over and over Lincoln declared that the implications of America's struggle would significantly affect not only the whole race of men then living but also the generations still to come. Were it not that Abraham Lincoln was so obviously and so firmly grounded in an understanding of his own imperfections and limits, one might be tempted to judge him to be unsettlingly grandiose about his perception of the role fate had chosen for him. But he was neither grandiose nor even inaccurate. The idea of republican democracy as embodied in the Constitution and inspired by the Declaration of Indepen-

---

90. Ralph G. Newman, "Lincoln and the Family of Man" in Newman, ed., *Lincoln for the Ages* (New York: Doubleday, 1960), 415–20.

dence would indeed have worldwide implications for the generations to come. As Frank J. Williams has pointed out: "Carl Sandburg was right when he said at the end of his oration before a joint session of the United States Congress, 'The people of many other countries take Lincoln now for their own. He belongs to them. . . . He had something they would like to see spread everywhere in the world . . . Democracy.'"[91]

Like the second President Bush for much of his life before he became president, Lincoln had limited familiarity with the rest of the world beyond the United States. He never set foot outside his own country, save for one brief visit to the Canadian side of Niagara Falls on his way to Washington to serve in Congress. During his lifetime his principal exposure to foreign cultures came from the words of Shakespeare and Robert Burns that he read, memorized, and loved to recite. Shakespeare in particular taught him a little about European history—enough so that when he rose to deliver the final, climactic speech of his debates with Stephen A. Douglas in 1858, Lincoln inveighed against

[T]he eternal struggle between these two principles—right and wrong—throughout the world. They are the two principles that have stood face to face from the beginning of time; and will ever continue to struggle. The one is the common right of humanity and the other the divine right of kings. It is the same principle in whatever shape it develops itself. It is the same spirit that says, "You work and toil and earn bread, and I'll eat it." No matter in what shape it comes, whether from the

91. Cuomo and Holzer, eds., *Lincoln on Democracy*, 351.

mouth of a king who seeks to bestride the people of his own nation and live by the fruit of their labor, or from one race of men as an apology for enslaving another race, it is the same tyrannical principle.[92]

Closer to home, Lincoln came to know refugees from the tumultuous European upheavals of 1848. He not only learned from them firsthand about the extent of tyranny overseas, but he also began working to recruit them to the new Republican Party. Lincoln even purchased a German-language newspaper to spread the Republican credo to new voters from Europe. Of course, when Stephen A. Douglas supposedly schemed to lure Irish-born voters from other states to cast their ballots for him in the race for the Senate against Lincoln, Republicans howled in protest. Yet Lincoln would never agree to embrace any movement that called for excluding "foreigners and Catholics." As he put it: "When it comes to this I should prefer emigrating to some country where they make no pretence of loving liberty—to Russia, for instance, where despotism can be taken pure, and without the base alloy of hypocrasy [sic]."[93]

Lincoln's "devotion to the principles of our free institutions was expressed again on the eve of Hungarian freedom fighter Louis Kossuth's visit to America in 1852. Lincoln helped draft a resolution that affirmed the "sacred principles of the laws of nature and of nations—principles held dear by the friends of freedom everywhere, and more especially by the people of these United States." The highest of these

---

92. *Collected Works*, 3:315.

93. Lincoln to Joshua Speed, August 24, 1855, in *Collected Works*, 2:323.

principles, Lincoln believed, was "the supremacy of the people," both here and abroad.94

The Republican Party platform on which Lincoln ran for president did not even mention foreign policy. Once in the White House, however, he was forced to educate himself swiftly: global interdependence was already an unavoidable reality. To his experienced secretary of state, William H. Seward, he delegated the routine of maintaining correspondence with foreign leaders. But when the administration faced its first and perhaps worst foreign crisis, Lincoln dealt with the matter directly. He demonstrated that he knew when to be aggressive and when to be conciliatory—a valuable skill for any president, even one engaged in leading the nation in war.

The crisis began in November 1861 when a Union ship, the *San Jacinto*, stopped a British mail packet called the *Trent* that was bound for England with two Confederate envoys on board headed for diplomatic posts in London. The Union captain seized the emissaries and detained them, and the British government responded by threatening war over this breach of diplomatic immunity. Faced with an ultimatum, Lincoln might have used the crisis to encourage reunification at home; a threat by a common foreign foe, some had argued, would effectively end the rebellion. Lincoln would have none of it. He even considered the idea of turning the dispute over to a neutral third-party country for arbitration. Ultimately, when he saw no way out of the crisis, although he was fearful that public opinion would turn against him for failing to take Britain's dare, Lincoln released the envoys. In the end, the crisis

94. *Collected Works*, 2:115–16.

was quickly forgotten, a war averted, and a lesson learned by those presidents wise enough to know their history.

Lincoln never became skilled at diplomatic protocol. He welcomed ambassadors and aristocrats to the White House at formal receptions, but he never learned the language of diplomacy or took with complete seriousness the epaulets and waxed mustaches parading before him. Lincoln, nevertheless, impressed most of the foreign visitors. "It was strange to me," one British visitor admitted, "to witness the terms of perfect equality on which he appeared to be with everybody." Moreover, the visitor conceded, "the tone in which he spoke of England was, for an American, unusually fair and candid."[95]

The 1864 platform, unlike the party credo published four years earlier, reflected Lincoln's growing awareness of the world about him. Republicans agreed to encourage foreign immigration and "the asylum of the oppressed of all nations . . . which in the past has added so much to the wealth, development of resources, and increase of power to this nation." At the same time, it resolved to show no "indifference" to the attempt of any "monarchial" European power to menace peace with an attack on the Western Hemisphere. Such interference, Lincoln's party believed, would not only threaten America, but the "interdependence of their own country." Lincoln could draw lines in the sand, too, when it came to maintaining peace and preserving democratic institutions."[96]

---

95. Edward Dicey, quoted in Harold Holzer, ed., *Lincoln as I Knew Him* (New York: Algonquin Books, 1999), 121–22.

96. Appendix to David E. Long, *The Jewel of Liberty: Abraham Lincoln's Re-election and the End of Slavery* (Mechanicsburg, Penn.: Stackpole Books, 1994), 281.

To Leo Tolstoy in distant Russia, Lincoln seemed "a humanitarian as broad as the whole world." And when Lincoln died, tributes poured in from the very monarchs whose totalitarian rule Lincoln had so vigorously contested. Poland lauded him as "a victim, a martyr, of the great cause" of liberty. And from Italy, Garibaldi eulogized the fallen president as the "heir of the aspirations of Christ." Throughout Europe, artists created mass-produced pictures that became as popular there as the depictions now treasured by his American admirers.[97]

The extraordinary metamorphosis in world public opinion was perhaps best expressed by Tom Taylor, the English writer whose play, *Our American Cousin*, Lincoln was watching when John Wilkes Booth pulled the trigger that ended the president's life. Lamented Taylor:

> *The Old World and the New, from sea to sea,*
> *Utter one voice of sympathy and shame!*
> *Sore heart, so stopped when it at last beat high,*
> *Sad life, cut short just as its triumph came.*[98]

As Lincoln knew, American self-preservation rested solely with the American people. But even in an age when distances between nations seemed vast and unbridgeable, Lincoln believed "that favor or disfavor of foreign nations might have material influence" in determining America's future. "A fair examination of history," he maintained, "has

---

97. Cuomo and Holzer, eds. *Lincoln on Democracy*, xxxiv, xxxviii–xxxix.
98. *Punch*, May 6, 1865, reprinted in Herbert Mitgang, ed., *Abraham Lincoln: A Press Portrait* (Chicago: Quadrangle Books, 1971), 489.

seemed to authorize a belief that the past action and influences of the United States" [would be] beneficent towards mankind." On this belief Lincoln based his attitude toward the rest of the world. It won him something precious, something worth aspiring to even now: "the forbearance of nations." Not by force—but by example.[99]

George W. Bush's early years as president were marked by an apparent eagerness to separate our nation from "entangling" alliances as George Washington had first urged. Bush rejected the Kyoto Protocol, attempts to create international justice tribunals, and existing weapons agreements; and then he engaged in a serious contretemps with France, Germany, and much of the rest of the world over how to deal with Iraq. His disrespect for the United Nations was apparent and antagonistic at times. When one of Bush's principal spokesmen on the Iraq situation, Secretary of Defense Donald Rumsfeld, dismissed France and Germany, the two strongest nations in Europe, as the "old Europe" and distinguished them from the "new Europe" of nations like Poland and a handful of struggling countries, the president's acquiescence made the insult even more meaningful. After the American attack on Iraq was over, the United States at first refused to share the burdens of reconstruction with "old Europe." This wasn't because we didn't need the help. Our miscalculation of the cost in dollars, personnel, and time was already a major embarrassment to the administration. Rather, the apparent reason for the rejection was that we did not wish to share the economic boon expected from

---

99. Lincoln to the workingmen of Manchester, England, January 19, 1863, in *Collected Works*, 6:64.

our ability to direct work to American companies and to share the benefits of Iraq's huge oil resources.

Thereafter, as it became clear that the American occupation was not going to achieve its objective of reconstruction without more troops and a lot more time, the president tried to convince some of the "old Europe" to help. Unsurprisingly, their first reaction was negative.

Perhaps the most significant aspect of President Bush's reactionary impulse of "America first . . . and maybe even only" is that it defies the one great and obvious reality in today's world—a reality that Lincoln recognized nearly 150 years ago. The reality is that the world grows every day more interconnected and interdependent because of rapidly developing technology, transportation, and communication. It is clear, even from the most superficial reading of world history, that no nation—not even the superpower known as the United States—can achieve its full potential alone. Nor should it try to. With each new step in our history, as technological advancement narrows the physical distances that separate people and nations, we become more cognizant of this reality. The Great Depression demonstrated that we had to do a better job of accommodating the interconnectedness and interdependence of our own population by using our government more intelligently and imaginatively to survive. The same recognition that the world grows up to something better through integration and not fragmentation directed our foreign policy as well. The failed League of Nations recognized the need for instruments of international unity but was unable to make it work. The United Nations, while by no means flawless in its execution, has been markedly more successful.

Perhaps the most dramatic example of our acceptance of an idea as pragmatically essential even though it's not emotionally satisfying is the Marshall Plan and the programs to restore Japan after the Second World War. Were any of America's enemies more profoundly hated than the Nazis, who slaughtered millions of innocent human beings? Or the Japanese who started their war against us with the brutal sneak attack on Pearl Harbor? But still, after we defeated them, we spent billions of dollars to restore them to productivity, not out of compassion alone but because we needed these parts of the world for trade and because we were concerned by the potential chaos that might be caused by their devastation.

The need for that kind of intelligent mutuality is greater now than it has been for a long time, both as a matter of defensive policy and as a positive progressive policy to strengthen the weaker parts of the planet for their sake and ours. It is obvious that force alone will not be enough to defeat terrorism. If it were, the war would already be over. We need to help replace Saddam Hussein's and the Taliban's tyranny with some form of fairly representative, market-oriented, democratic governments in Iraq and Afghanistan. We also must work more effectively to create an enduring peace for the Israelis and the Palestinians, to allay the fears and alleviate the anger and pain of millions of people in the Middle East through aggressive and generous assistance, and to discredit the poisonous propaganda being fomented and distributed in the madrassas. While we are doing that, we must find a way to control the frightening proliferation of the nuclear weapons that we first unleashed nearly sixty years ago.

It is obvious we cannot do it alone despite all of our tremendous power. Nor can we do it with "crisis-driven coalitions of the willing by themselves" as was so aptly pointed out by Chuck Hagel, the highly respected Republican senator from Nebraska in October 2003.[100]

Today, when we need global cooperation the most, our credibility is at a low point because of our perceived arrogance, unilateralism, and bellicosity.

Lincoln did not know much about diplomatic protocol, but he knew how to make friends with foreign countries by showing respect. A lesson so simple should have been easy enough to learn for a Republican administration that likes to think of itself as a follower of the great leader, but so far it has failed to do so. The few glimmers of light and hope coming from our State Department are barely visible in the shadows created by angry clouds from the Capitol. Secretary of State Colin Powell's Millennium Challenge Account and Middle East Partnership Initiative are by design instruments of cooperation and assistance to needy people in the Middle East, but these plans have not yet been forcefully utilized as President Bush devotes himself to the work coming out of the Defense Department instead.

This combination of pragmatism and compassion has always marked our greatest leaders and wisest policies. Lincoln was a unique embodiment of those qualities in all that he did as president. He set a standard for all presidents and other leaders that they are not currently living up to. Among his most notable presidential papers were his letters to

---

100. James Traub, "The Party of the Strong," *New York Times Magazine*, January 4, 2004: 31.

workingmen's groups in Manchester, England, and New York City, in which, according to J. G. Randall, he showed a "basic Americanism" in his concern for the aspirations and needs of working people worldwide and in his hope that American actions could continue to be "beneficent towards mankind" everywhere by promoting "the ultimate and universal triumph of justice, humanity and freedom." As he wrote in his letter to the New York group: "The strongest bond of human sympathy . . . should be one uniting all working people, of all nations, and tongues, and kindreds. Property is the fruit of labor—property is desirable—is a positive good in the world. . . . Let not him who is houseless pull down the house of another; but let him labor diligently and build one himself, thus by example assuring that his own shall be safe from violence when built."[101]

This instinct for universality, this appreciation for the interconnectedness and interdependence of all parts of the globe that should make the desire for integration and cooperation stronger than the desire for aloofness and hegemony, are clearly not as strong a part of our current administration's outlook and *modus operandi* as they should be.

"We stand at once as the wonder and admiration of the whole world," Lincoln observed five years before he became president. Lincoln also believed that America was, as Ralph Newman put it, "a trustee for all humanity." Americans were the "almost chosen people," blessed with vast territory,

101. January 19, 1863, in *Collected Works*, 6:64; March 21, 1864, ibid., 7:259–60; J. G. Randall, *Lincoln the Liberal Statesman* (London: Eyre & Spottiswoode, Ltd., 1947), 189.

endless resources, and unlimited opportunity to set an example for the world based on the ideas of freedom and equality. Perhaps that is why Lincoln ended his last great speech by advocating not only "peace among ourselves" but also "with all nations."[102]

102. Speech at Kalamazoo, August 27, 1856, in *Collected Works*, 2:364; Second inaugural address, March 4, 1865, in ibid., 8:333; Newman, *Lincoln for the Ages*, 416–17.

Religion

ABRAHAM LINCOLN used the language of religion freely and eloquently, most notably in a remarkable second inaugural address that was filled with Biblical references. "Woe unto the world because of offences," the president intoned that day, quoting from the book of Matthew. "The judgments of the Lord are true and righteous altogether," he added, quoting Psalm 19. The sun burst through persistent clouds as he spoke, convincing many eyewitnesses to the spectacle that the Almighty Himself was blessing the proceedings.[103] In the private sphere, Lincoln's attitude toward, and relationship with, organized religion was far more complicated. In his Illinois years, he paid for a reserved pew, which his wife customarily used. But Lincoln rarely used that pew or any other; there is no indication that he considered himself part of any formal religion or single church or that he believed in Jesus Christ as God, though several early biographers went out of their way to so in-

---

103. *Collected Works*, 8:333.

sist.[104] Indeed, there is no evidence that he ever utilized the Bible to articulate a theological view that would have made him seem either a Christian or a Jew.

Early in Lincoln's career, opponents tried spreading the rumor that he was a nonbeliever, an infidel. But his admirers laughed heartily when Lincoln's opponent in the congressional election of 1846, Peter Cartwright, asked at a campaign rally—revival meeting that everyone who expected to go to heaven stand up and be counted. Next he asked those in attendance who expected to go to hell to rise, too. When Lincoln stubbornly remained seated, Reverend Cartwright is said to have inquired where his opponent intended to go. "If it is all the same to you," came the reply, "I intend to go to Congress."[105]

In a more serious vein, Lincoln answered the whispering campaign against him in 1846 by issuing a printed reply in the form of a campaign handbill. He was not, he maintained, an "enemy of religion" or "an open scoffer at Christianity." True, he was "not a member of any Christian Church," but he would never "insult the feelings, and injure the morals, of the community," he maintained. He summed up the evolution of his own belief system this way:

---

104. The most prominent early example of such treatments was J. G. Holland's *The Life of Abraham Lincoln* (Springfield, Mass.: Gurdon Bill, 1866). Historian Mark E. Neely, Jr., has particularly pointed to Holland's contention that Lincoln's efforts to save the Union and end slavery were best described as the labors of "a simple, honest, Christian heart." See Neely, *The Abraham Lincoln Encyclopedia* (New York: McGraw-Hill, 1982), 149.

105. The legend is recounted in Paul Findley's *A. Lincoln: The Crucible of Congress* (New York: Crown Publishers, 1979), 34.

It is true that in early life I was inclined to believe in what I understand is called the "Doctrine of Necessity"—that is, that the human mind is impelled to action, or held in rest by some power, over which the mind itself has no control.[106]

Lincoln did enjoy listening to good preachers, even while campaigning and when he was president. He went out of his way to visit Brooklyn twice during his 1860 campaign stop in New York City—the trip during which he delivered his Cooper Union address—where he listened to the sermons of the noted minister Henry Ward Beecher at Plymouth Church. But it is likely that Lincoln was attracted to Beecher more because of his reputation as an abolitionist than as a man of God. As president, Lincoln attended Sunday worship services, but as historian Ronald C. White has recently pointed out, he came to prefer coming in secret to midweek prayer meetings, never occupying a pew but rather sequestering himself in the minister's private office, door ajar so he could hear the sermons. He preferred the New York Avenue Presbyterian church, he told a friend, because its pastor "don't preach politics [sic]." Just as he held politics separate from religion, he, in turn, wanted a church "whose clergyman holds himself aloof from politics."[107]

Lincoln never quite decided, while the Civil War raged,

---

106. *Collected Works,* 1:382. Lincoln contended in the handbill that he had not believed in this kind of fatalistic approach for some five years.

107. Ronald C. White, Jr., *Lincoln's Greatest Speech: The Second Inaugural* (New York: Simon & Schuster, 2002), 138, 141.

whether the Almighty blessed the efforts of the Union or the Confederacy. The problem confounded and distressed him, and he gave it much thought. "In great contests each party claims to act in accordance with the will of God," he concluded in jottings he composed six months after the death of his young son but never made public. "Both *may* be, and one *must* be, wrong," he acknowledged. "God can not be *for* and *against* the same thing at the same time." Later, at his second inauguration, he conceded publicly that both sides "pray to the same God" and that each "invokes His aid against the other." His only answer to this conundrum was "judge not that we be not judged."[108]

Although he was thought of as a Christian by many contemporaries because of his frequent public references to the Bible, Lincoln refused ever to acknowledge any affiliation with any formal religion. Just three months before his second inauguration Lincoln had suggested his lack of affiliation in an article he asked a journalist to print titled "The President's Last, Shortest, and Best Speech":

> On thursday of last week two ladies from Tennessee came before the President asking the release of their husbands held as prisoners of war at Johnson's Island. They were put off till Friday, when they came again; and were again put off to saturday. At each of the interviews one of the ladies urged that her husband was a religious man. On saturday the President ordered the release of the prisoners, and then said to this lady "You say your husband is a religious man; tell him when you

108. *Collected Works*, 5:403; 8:333.

meet him, that I say I am not much of a judge of religion, but that, in my opinion, the religion that sets men
to rebel and fight against their government, because, as
they think, that government does not sufficiently help
some men to eat their bread on the sweat of *other* men's
faces, is not the sort of religion upon which people can
get to heaven!"[109]

On another occasion Lincoln acknowledged to Harry C.
Deming, a congressman from Connecticut, why he had
never joined any church and why his fundamental spiritual
disposition was simple and profound:

> I have never united myself to any church, because I have
> found difficulty in giving my assent, without mental
> reservation, to the long, complicated statements of
> Christian doctrine which characterize their Articles of
> Belief and Confessions of the Faith. When any church
> will inscribe over its altar, as its sole qualification for
> membership . . . the Saviour's condensed statement of
> both Law and Gospel, "Thou shalt love the Lord thy
> God with all thy heart, and with all thy soul, and with
> all thy mind, and thy neighbor as thyself," that church
> will I join with all my heart and all my soul.[110]

After Lincoln's death, eulogists elevated him to the status
of a latter-day Christian martyr. He had been shot on Good
Friday, and the coincidence was not lost on the preachers

---

109. December 6, 1864, in *Collected Works*, 8:154–55.
110. Francis B. Carpenter, *Six Months at the White House with Abraham Lincoln* (Hurd
and Houghton, 1866) 190. The Biblical quote is from the book of Matthew.

who told their congregations on that "Black Easter" of mourning that Lincoln, like Jesus, had died for the people's sins. In synagogues, too, rabbis found holiness in Lincoln's life and sacrifice: He was a modern Moses who had, in the words from Leviticus, proclaimed liberty throughout the land but who had not quite reached the promised land himself. Naturally enough, the ministers and rabbis who preached that weekend needed to proclaim Lincoln a believer before they could make him a deity. "I doubt if any President has ever shown such a trust in God," announced the minister who presided at his burial. God blessed the Union's efforts, he insisted, "because we were trying to do right."[111]

But while the vast majority of preachers stressed what they believed to be Lincoln's "faith," a few were emboldened enough to openly regret what one called the late president's failure to "make a public confession . . . of faith in the Lord Jesus Christ." One minister in Lincoln's hometown conceded that Lincoln "had never been known as a professor of religion."[112] Faith in God and fealty to a single religion were surely not the same thing—even in Lincoln's age of almost uniform conformity and church loyalty.

In a simple but certainly not simplistic way, Lincoln's statement to Deming embodied his faith—as well as the principal idea upon which rests most of the many religions

111. Funeral oration by Matthew Simpson, Springfield, Illinois, May 4, 1865, in Braden, *Building the Myth*, 83. For comparisons to Moses, see David B. Chesebrough, *No Sorrow Like Our Sorrow: Northern Protestant Ministers and the Assassination of Abraham Lincoln* (Kent, Ohio: Kent State University Press, 1994) 35–37. The standard reference on Jewish eulogies is Emanuel Hertz, *Tribute of the Synagogue* (New York: Bloch Publishing, 1927).

112. Chesebrough, *No Sorrow Like Our Sorrow*, 28–31.

practiced in our nation today. It does so without any of the more intricate and elusive concepts required by various orthodoxies that call upon their believers to accept truths as a matter of faith or revelation. In effect, it is a statement of natural law, or as it is described in the Declaration of Independence, the law prescribed by "Nature's God."

President Bush and right-wing Republican advocates have raised the issue of religion frequently in recent years, asserting an increasingly specific and dogmatic brand of religious action. They advocate direct subsidies to formal, so-called faith-based religious groups; claim that Democrats are biased against Catholics for objecting to pro-life judicial candidates or the posting of the Ten Commandments on public buildings, and insist from time to time that their Republican principles are based on the teachings of Jesus Christ.

That kind of politics clearly would not have appealed to Lincoln. Although not many church-state issues reached the courts in his day, had Lincoln been confronted with a federally proposed law purporting to deal with abortion, stem-cell retrieval, contraceptives, or homosexuality, he likely would have answered the question not by applying a religious test but by applying secular logic. For him, the question in each case would be, Would the statute violate anyone's rights under the Constitution and, if not, is it protective or destructive of the common good?

Surely Lincoln, who valued above all prescriptions the insistence on equality and the rights in the Declaration of Independence, would have been strongly protective of the First Amendment right of every individual to privately follow his or her specific religious beliefs. And aware as he was of the need not to prefer one religious group over another or over nonbelievers, he would be equally protective of the First Amendment prohibition against the government establishment of any religion or religions in general.

Modern proposals that prohibit all removals of a fertilized egg from the moment of conception onward no matter what the purpose or circumstance, would result in the banning of all abortion and embryonic stem-cell removal. The basis for such proposals is the religious belief that life begins at the moment of conception and that the destruction of the fertilized egg amounts to the killing of a human being. That is President Bush's position, and it is usually the platform posture of Republican presidential candidates. Lincoln certainly would not have felt obliged to push for legislation or court rulings that would have prohibited all abortions—including those necessary to save the life of the mother—on the religious premise that life begins at conception, especially since that is not even a conclusion supported by a consensus of religions.

On the other hand, when expert medical evidence states that a fetus has grown to the point of viability in the womb and the Supreme Court concludes that at this point it cannot be destroyed without proof that it must be done to save the life or health of the mother, as the Supreme Court did in *Roe v. Wade,* Lincoln would probably have felt compelled to honor that decision as long as it stood since it was based on more than religious belief.

Lincoln would have done everything he could to protect the right of true believers to live by their own religious principles. No one would be compelled to use stem-cell research or its products, just as no one would ever be compelled to have an abortion or to use contraceptives in violation of their religious beliefs. Lincoln also would have respected the right of believers to advocate for changes in our civil law that correspond with their particular view of morality. But Lincoln would have understood, too, that before this pluralistic nation could adopt religious beliefs or strongly held moral commitments as the secular law of the land, it would have to be persuaded by more than religious orthodoxy or the presumed authority of religious leaders. In the end, in Lincoln's America, laws adopted by our political system would arise out of consensus not out of the dictates of religious credos. And once adopted, they would prevail as the law of the land no matter how much in disagreement they might be with the personal religious beliefs of some Americans.

If Lincoln shunned orthodoxy, he embraced ecumenism. Lincoln passed several grueling tests of his tolerance during the Civil War. Although prevailing law required all military chaplains to be Christians, Lincoln named Rabbi Jacob Frankel of Philadelphia the first Jewish chaplain in American history. Later in the war, when General Ulysses S. Grant issued a reprehensible order banning "Jews, as a class" from territory under his control, Lincoln had the edict overturned. As he told Rabbi Stephen Wise of New York, he saw "no distinction between Jews and Gentiles."[113]

To Lincoln, the separation between church and state was inviolate. Warned that some Missouri ministers were preaching disloyalty to the Union, the president refused to silence them, maintaining "that the U.S. government must not . . . undertake to run the churches." And he added this

---

113. See Harold Holzer, *Lincoln and the Jews: The Last Best Hope of Earth* (Los Angeles: Skirball Cultural Center, 2002).

statement of principle—worthy as an example to all future presidents—"I have never interfered, nor thought of interfering as to who shall or shall not preach in any church."[114]

It is abundantly clear today that neither President Bush nor American religious believers have made their case for when life begins persuasively enough to win the day on the issues of abortion and stem-cell use. Many Americans, vividly aware of the millions of tragic victims of Alzheimer's, Parkinson's, cancer, and spinal-cord injuries, believe embryonic stem-cell research may provide cures and will insist that Congress act to realize that potential. If they do and the president were to veto such a bill, he would have to provide a more consistent and persuasive rationale than he has so far or suffer the political consequences. Lincoln would have signed such a bill.

Religion's place in our system of government is an elusive topic. The legal precedents and social attitudes that attend it are complex, shifting, and sometimes contradictory. Even trying to define the basic words can be an adventure. Most nonlawyers—and maybe even lawyers, too—would assume that the word *religion* necessarily implies a belief in God and perhaps even monotheism. Not so. *Religion* has been defined by the Supreme Court to include belief systems such as secular humanism that, by and large, reject the notion of God. *God* is an even more difficult concept to capture in words. *Black's Law Dictionary* doesn't even try. Some religious authorities say God is too big a reality to be literally embodied. Maybe that's why it appears nowhere in the law of the land—the Constitution. In the Declaration of Independence, which is not a law and therefore not subjected to

114. Lincoln to Oliver D. Filley, December 22, 1863, in *Collected Works*, 7:85–86.

rigorous interpretation and enforcement, the word *God* appears only in the context of natural law—"Laws of Nature and of Nature's God."

It has always seemed to me that language deserves more attention than it has received. Two of the basic principles of natural law—derived from our nature and from human reason without the benefit of revelation or a willing suspension of disbelief—are shared by most, if not all, of our nation's religions—whether they specifically include God or not. In effect, President Lincoln summed them up in his comments to Congressman Henry Deming. These principles are the obligation that binds all human beings to recognize their equal entitlement to respect and dignity and the necessity of human beings to work together to repair and improve the world around us.

Judaism, the earliest of our monotheistic religions, calls these two ideas *tzedakah* and *tikkun olam*. Christianity, founded by a Jew, was built on precisely the same principles. Jesus' words, approximately, were "Love one another as you love yourself for the love of me; and I am truth. The truth is God has created the world but not completed it, and it is your mission to collaborate in its completion."

Indeed, in a number of places, the great writings of Christianity and Judaism describe those two simple ideas as "the whole law." The *Qur'an* honors both of these basic principles, as do the holy scriptures of other major religions.

It seemed to Lincoln, Alexis de Tocqueville, and many others that these two basic religious precepts are of great benefit to our nation and can be even more beneficial if focused on and stressed. What better guidance can our increasingly interconnected and interdependent world be given than this intelligent acceptance of the benefit of mutuality and commitment to promoting a moral and healthy society together? Nor is it terribly difficult to nail down these two natural law–religious principles to the procrustean bed of reality dealt with day to day by government. Much of the discussion and debate concerning government's role in our life revolves around the competition between the virtues of individualism and community. Lincoln reconciled these virtues by living the biblical instruction he had quoted to Henry Deming. His religious principles come down to this: We need to love one another, to come together to create a good society, and to use that mutuality discreetly in order to gain the benefits of community without sacrificing the importance of individual freedom and responsibility. Such a philosophy requires what, in scholar William J. Wolf's words, constitutes "a dynamic for responsible action" by individuals on earth.[115] The underlying idea is "malice toward none" and "charity for all"—*tzedakah* and *tikkun olam*. In these admittedly broad terms, this idea would be good government for the twenty-first century and a concept that should also be inviting to people who think of themselves as religious.

To Lincoln, the holiest and certainly the noblest of causes was that of "establishing and maintaining civil liberty." "God knows best," Lincoln was willing to concede in his moments of fatalism; but, anticipating the words of John F. Kennedy a century later, he insisted that here on earth "mortals . . . must work earnestly in the best light He gives us."[116]

---

115. William J. Wolf, *The Religion of Abraham Lincoln*, orig. pub. as *The Almost Chosen People* (New York: The Seabury Press, 1963), 190.

116. *Collected Works*, 1:114; 7:535. The latter statement came in a letter to the Quaker leader, Mrs. Elizah P. Gurney, on September 4, 1864.

The Supreme Court

ABRAHAM LINCOLN was a superb lawyer who rose to the top of the Illinois legal profession as a courtroom advocate. He had all the classical lawyer's gifts: high intelligence; a mind that insisted on logic, reason, and orderliness; abundant common sense; and a spectacular gift for written and spoken communication. All of this is evident in the many volumes of his speeches and writings that have been admired for years all over the globe and in the documents painstakingly assembled more recently by the Lincoln Legal Papers project in Springfield, Illinois.

Lincoln was an advocate who could make almost any legal position sound plausible (indeed, he once represented the owner of an escaped slave under the heinous fugitive slave laws), but he also—at least in his earlier years—had a near reverence for the letter and spirit of the Constitution and the rule of law. That passion was brilliantly displayed in his often-cited address on "the perpetuation of our political institutions" before the Young Men's Lyceum of Springfield, Illinois, in 1838. It was his first major speech, and his words that day are worth remembering:

[L]et every American pledge his life, his property, and his sacred honor;—let every man remember that to violate the law, is to trample on the blood of his father, and to tear the character [or charter] of his own, and his children's liberty. Let reverence for the laws, be breathed by every American mother, to the lisping babe, that prattles on her lap—let it be taught in schools, in seminaries, and in colleges;—let it be written in Primmers, spelling books and in Almanacs;—let it be preached from the pulpit, proclaimed in legislative halls, and enforced in the courts of justice. And, in short, let it become the *political religion* of the nation . . . bad laws, if they exist, should be repealed as soon as possible, still while they continue in force, for the sake of example, they should be religiously observed.[117]

In what many historians have noted as a stunning coincidence, Lincoln, during the course of this address, urged the people to be steadfast always, to keep the law strong, and to apply it in order to prevent a future tyrant—a "towering genius"—from seeking glory for himself by violating the law, "whether at the expense of emancipating slaves, or enslaving freemen." Emancipating slaves, of course, is precisely what the towering Lincoln (standing six feet four inches) eventually ordered.[118]

As historian David Herbert Donald has pointed out, Lincoln in his earlier years looked constantly to reason for

117. *Collected Works,* 1:112.
118. Ibid., 1:114.

guidance in his own turbulent life and "found stability in the law and in the Constitution." But then, Donald adds, after the United States Supreme Court issued its decision in *Dred Scott v. Sandford* in 1857, Lincoln "could no longer have unqualified faith in either." Instead, he turned to the "Declaration of Independence with its promise of liberty for all . . . as the . . . premise on which all his other political beliefs rested." To Lincoln, the *Dred Scott* decision was "based on assumed historical facts which were not really true." The Court was "insisting . . . that Negroes were no part of the people for whom was made, the Declaration of Independence, or the Constitution of the United States." If the framers "could rise from their graves," Lincoln charged, they would not recognize the original documents. He insisted that Jefferson and Jackson, both Democrats, shared his opposition to "the binding authority of Supreme Court decisions." Only if decisions boasted unanimity, the absence of partisan bias, and "accordance with legal public expectation" did citizens have to "acquiesce in them." But if a decision was "wanting in all these claims to the public confidence, it is not resistance, it is not factious, it is not even disrespectful, to treat it as not having yet quite established a settled doctrine for the country."[119]

Lincoln's fear was that the *Dred Scott* decision doomed African Americans to a perpetual "prison house," which the executive branch, the legislature, and now the judiciary had constructed "with a lock of a hundred keys, which can never be unlocked without the concurrence of every key . . . [making] the impossibility of . . . [their] escape" complete. The

119. Donald, *Lincoln*, 239; *Collected Works*, 2:403–4

Dred Scott case and the principle of judicial supremacy shook Lincoln's commitment to the letter of the Constitution, and the South's secession nearly uprooted it. That was evidenced in his numerous suspensions of the Bill of Rights during the Civil War and to a lesser extent—but still undisguisedly—in the manner in which he approached the appointment of justices to the Supreme Court.[120]

In just four years and a few weeks as president, Lincoln appointed five men to the Supreme Court, including a chief justice. He entered office with an enviable three vacancies to fill—one left by death, one by disloyalty to the Union, and one by his predecessor's reluctance to appoint a new judge. One of the earliest vacancies occurred for an unprecedented reason: an associate justice from Alabama resigned to go south, pledging loyalty to the rebellion and the Confederacy.

Facing a court deadlocked at 3–3 in possible support for any war he might wage to put down rebellion, Lincoln named Noah H. Swayne of Ohio, Samuel F. Miller of Iowa, and David Davis of Illinois to the court, all in 1862, and Stephen J. Field of California in 1863. All of his nominees hailed from states whose voters had supported Lincoln in the 1860 presidential election. Miller grew up, like Lincoln, on a Kentucky farm, became a pro-internal improvement Whig, and championed economic opportunity.[121] Davis, moreover, was a longtime friend, a legal associate from Illinois, and later the executor of Lincoln's estate. They had

---

120. Speech in Springfield, June 26, 1857, in *Collected Works*, 2:404.
121. Michael A. Ross, *Justice of Shattered Dreams: Samuel Freeman Miller and the Supreme Court During the Civil War Era* (Baton Rouge: Louisiana State University Press 2003), 77–78.

known each other well enough to travel the judicial eighth circuit together, staying at the same inns and boarding-houses. In addition, Davis had served as Lincoln's campaign manager during the 1860 presidential race. The runner-up for Lincoln's judicial nomination, most historians agree, was Orville Hickman Browning, another of the president's old cronies from back home in Illinois. Mary Lincoln could not resist weighing in, urging her husband to reject Browning for Davis. And yet another Illinois friend, Leonard Swett, wrote to Lincoln on Davis's behalf to remind him: "Should not a man in power remember those men, who throughout his life have been as true as steel to him?"[122]

Vacancies notwithstanding, Lincoln inexplicably waited more than ten months before naming his first Supreme Court justice—then another seven months to name the second. He was perhaps in no hurry to name judges to a bench for which he had so often expressed disrespect. The president also wanted to prevent the judges from scattering to their respective judicial circuits, where they might make rulings at odds with administration policy. As Lincoln put it:

> I have so far forborne making nominations to fill these vacancies . . . Two of the outgoing judges resided within the States now overrun by revolt [not that Lincoln was obligated to replace them with judges from the same geographic areas of the country] so that if successors

122. Swett to Lincoln, January 15, 1862, Abraham Lincoln Papers, Library of Congress (microfilm); Browning's quest for the appointment detailed in David Herbert Donald, *We Are Lincoln Men: Abraham Lincoln and His Friends* (New York: Simon & Schuster, 2003), 122–27.

were appointed in the same localities, they could not now serve upon their circuits; and many of the most competent men there, probably would not take the personal hazard of accepting to serve, even here, upon the supreme bench. I have been unwilling to throw all the appointments northward, thus disabling myself from doing justice to the south on the return of peace.[123]

Arguing that "the country generally has outgrown our present judicial system," Lincoln urged in his first annual message to Congress that either circuit courts be abolished entirely and their business left to district courts or that Supreme Court justices be entirely "relieved" of their responsibility for sitting on the circuit. Lincoln's apparently sincere concern for these difficult demands on the judges' time and energy eventually resulted in much-needed reforms of the circuit system. Moreover, Lincoln did reject suggestions by the radicals in his own party that the Court be abolished or suspended during the rebellion. "Let the Supreme Court be of convenient number," he insisted.[124]

Yet, instead of requiring legal training and judicial experience as primary qualifications for his Supreme Court appointments, Lincoln paid much attention to geography (the vacancy that Davis filled, for example, was generally conceded to "belong" to the president's home state of Illinois; the only question was which Illinois man would get the job). Lincoln demanded that nominees, notwithstanding the

---

123. From the first annual message to Congress, December 3, 1861, in *Collected Works*, 5:41.
124. Ibid., 41–42.

reluctance he had expressed to Congress the year before, hail from the loyal states and have the "right views" with respect to the difficult political decisions Lincoln had made and would be forced to make—many of which he accurately foresaw would eventually be subjected to review and ratification by the judiciary.[125]

Surely Lincoln's most difficult choice of all—and the most important one—was the selection of a chief justice to succeed the author of the *Dred Scott* decision, Maryland-born slave-owner Roger B. Taney, who died in 1864 at the age of eighty-seven after twenty-eight epochal years as chief.[126] He eventually selected his recently departed secretary of the treasury, Salmon P. Chase, whose intelligence, judgment, and reputation for legal ability were unchallenged but whose political loyalty Lincoln did not trust. A onetime rival for the Republican presidential nomination in 1860, Chase had been an effective cabinet officer—in fact he was one of the greatest treasury secretaries in American history; but he never lost his thirst for the presidency and, a few months before Taney's death, had encouraged his admirers to launch a campaign to replace Lincoln at the top of the ticket in the upcoming election. The bid failed. With Lincoln safely reelected, Chase no longer represented a political threat to the president. Lincoln did not elevate him to the court, as some myths have maintained, to get Chase out of his way.

125. David M. Silver, *Lincoln's Supreme Court* (Urbana: University of Illinois Press, 1956), 57–59.
126. Taney's admirers in Annapolis later erected a statue in his honor outside the state capitol; more recently, in a poignant irony, modern Marylanders erected nearby a statue of a justice who the state had produced a century later: the first African American ever to serve on the high court, Thurgood Marshall.

Lincoln spent weeks wrestling with the choice, checking with politicians of various stripes, trying to anticipate to what extent Chase's conclusions as to the law might obstruct the decisions Lincoln had already made politically—and those he might have to make in the future. "Chase men say the place is promised to their *magnifico*," Lincoln's private secretary recorded in his diary. Meanwhile, the president's White House mailbag bulged with suggestions that he name Chase, or Frederick Fogg of Boston, or associate justice Noah Swayne.[127] He was not particularly worried about Chase knowing the law and applying it with classical legal appropriateness—he wanted someone who would advance his policies, not obstruct them the way Chief Justice Taney had in *Dred Scott* and other cases.

Since a vacancy already awaited the incoming president on the mostly Democratic bench led by Taney, and secession and Civil War were imminent, the question of how the Court would decide critical issues arising out of the war was an important one. At the same time, Lincoln and antislavery advocates were eager to take over the court to reverse the *Dred Scott* decision, just as today radical so-called pro-life forces are eager to overturn *Roe v. Wade* by adding politically conservative candidates to the bench. To a large extent Lincoln and his political operatives did not think of the Supreme Court as the separate and independent branch of the government it was supposed to be; rather, they sought to make it, to the extent they could, an extension of the presidency.

---

127. Michael Burlingame, ed., *Inside Lincoln's White House: The Complete Civil War Diary of John Hay* (Carbondale: Southern Illinois University Press, 1997), 241; Holzer, ed., *Dear Mr. Lincoln*, 273.

In his 1861 inaugural address, Lincoln had reluctantly accepted the Supreme Court's authority to decide the constitutionality of legislative statutes and executive actions established by *Marbury v. Madison* in 1803 by Chief Justice Marshall and his court. But he also made clear he would resist any Supreme Court decisions if he believed they transgressed the Court's proper sphere of authority and reached into government policy instead. He encouraged the justices to review and reverse their own "questionable" decisions and also suggested that the legislature should redo legislative efforts that had been stricken or adopt corrective legislation to undo Supreme Court "transgressions." Lincoln also reminded citizens of their right to a constitutional amendment undoing *Marbury v. Madison,* although he did not perceive it to be a realistic alternative.

Lincoln's two swearing-in ceremonies were historic for a number of reasons—one coming on the precipice of disunion and war, the other on the brink of reunion and peace. Also remarkable was the fact that, on both occasions, Lincoln took the oath from longtime enemies: first Taney, the author of the reviled *Dred Scott* decision, and then Chase, the eternally ambitious political foe. At his first inauguration, he made clear his belief in a higher authority than the Supreme Court over whose makeup he would soon exercise such control:

> I do not forget the position assumed by some, that constitutional questions are to be decided by the Supreme Court; nor do I deny that such decisions must be binding . . . And while it is obviously possible that such decision may be erroneous in any given case, still

the evil effect following it, being limited to that particular case, with the chance that it may be over-ruled, and never become a precedent for other cases, can better be borne than could the evils of a different practice. At the same time the candid citizen must confess that if the policy of the government, upon vital questions affecting the whole people, is to be irrevocably fixed by decisions of the Supreme Court, the instant they are made ... the people will have ceased, to be their own rulers, having, to that extent, practically resigned their government, into the hands of that eminent tribunal."[128]

In this astonishingly blunt public warning, Lincoln was laying the groundwork for his own prospective executive actions in defiance of the Supreme Court by seeding public opinion in favor of the proposition that the Court should be subject to the political system he led as president instead of being superior to it as *Marbury v. Madison* had held.

There was a great deal Lincoln did not know about what lay ahead for the nation and for himself, but his keen intelligence properly assessed the probability that unique problems might require unique exercises of presidential power to avoid disaster. Eventually, that came to pass with his suspensions of civil liberties and other decisions. His political prudence was rewarded by his having "friendly" justices in place.

Legal purists today will point out that the wall of separation between the judiciary and the other two branches of government should be impenetrable. The Court should be

---

128. *Collected Works*, 4:268.

uncontaminated by politics. That is why justices are not elected but appointed for life and cannot have their salaries reduced. Justices ideally would be selected on the basis of their legal ability, experience, ability to communicate, collegiality, honesty, and integrity. Their political views would be totally irrelevant since decisions in court cases ought not be made the way political decisions are made. Lincoln, before his presidency began, openly questioned "the binding political authority of Supreme Court decisions" and also worried about future judicial nominees being "catechized in advance." A Court "so constituted," he argued then, would be "prostituted beneath the contempt of all men."[129]

In the Supreme Court, the question for the justices is how a specific case arising out of a specific controversy should be decided. The ultimate criteria for rulings are whether the conduct in question was constitutional or in compliance with whatever statutes and precedents might be relevant. On the other hand, a political decision made by the legislative or the executive branches is based upon whatever logic, history, sociology, or other considerations move the mind of the executive or legislature. In an abortion case, for example, the question for the justices would not be the same as the question facing legislators confronted with a proposed law granting women choice with respect to some abortions. The question for a justice would be, Is a statute denying, or limiting choice, constitutional? The question for the legislator would be, Is the law useful, fair, intelligent, and productive for a common good? The same person who would vote against the right of abortion if he or she were a legislator

---

129. From a fragment written ca. August 1858, in *Collected Works*, 2:552.

might very well uphold it as constitutional if sitting as a justice. Or vice versa. To the legal purists, this is more than a nice technicality; it is an essential ingredient of the exquisite design in our Constitution of a balanced government.

Despite what would be deemed correct answers on a law-school examination with respect to these fundamental questions, it is clear that when nominating justices, many presidents have been less than reverential in applying strict compliance with the original intent of the Founding Fathers.

In choosing nominees for the federal courts in his first few years, President Bush has appeared to go out of his way to include candidates who have indicated that they favor ending or curtailing abortion and that they support other political objectives that have not been accomplished by the political branches of government but might yet be addressed by the judiciary. If one could believe that these candidates could ignore their political opinions once they were serving as justices and could decide the cases objectively, then the fact that they held these political positions would serve as no impediment or inducement to selecting them.

The obvious reality is, however, that many of the senators who will be required to vote on confirmation are, in fact, persuaded that the candidates do indeed intend to use their judicial positions to achieve their political ends. Therefore, his opponents see President Bush's selections as an attempt to pack the courts with judges who would give him the kind of political support that he boasts has been provided by Supreme Court justices Antonin Scalia and Clarence Thomas. Especially after *Bush v. Gore* made George W. Bush president although more Americans voted for Al Gore, this prospect frightens many Americans and many senators and accounts for the occasional logjam in the senate confirmation process.

Constitutional purists would consider Bush's attempt to play politics with judicial nominations an offense against the fundamental design of our Constitution. But, as disappointing as it may be to the legal purist, the appointment of justices to the Supreme Court, like the conduct of presidents in times of war or other emergencies and Congress's reluctance to insist on its right and duty to declare war if war is to be conducted by the nation, has fallen into a category of acceptable departures from strict constitutionality. This is a triumph of practical politics over constitutional orthodoxy and amounts to a kind of silent, unauthorized rewriting of the rules by political authorities, but this is apparently not sufficiently offensive to the general public to warrant political reconsideration. Virtually all the presidents who have had the opportunity to appoint justices have put their assumptions about the candidates' political views first—or at least toward the top—on the list of qualifications, and they probably will continue to do that in the future as well.

President Bush's attempt to add to the courts judges and justices who would give him political support is not much different than the actions of Lincoln, Franklin Roosevelt, and most other presidents who had the chance to make appointments. Fortunately for the purists and the country, it has often been the case that after presidents have succeeded in getting their favorites on the Court and then expect them to accommodate their political desires, the justices have been good judges instead of predictably political ones.

Dwight Eisenhower rued appointing Earl Warren to the high court; Warren turned out to be the most progressive chief in justice history. No one expected Hugo Black, a former Ku Klux Klan member, to turn into a liberal positivist or President Kennedy's sole appointment, Byron White, to be such a difficult obstacle to interpretations dear to the Warren court. The first President Bush no doubt chides himself for nominating the progressive David Souter to the bench.

And, had he lived, no one would have been more surprised than Abraham Lincoln to learn who wrote the majority opinion in the watershed test of presidential powers in the Civil War, *Ex parte Milligan* (1866), that rejected Lincoln's action. "Martial rule," wrote the justice, "can never exist where the courts are open." The author was Lincoln's old friend, adviser, and campaign manager, David Davis.

We can only hope that history repeats itself.

Race

MOST OF THE Lincoln years as president were consumed by
the Civil War and the slavery issue that precipitated it. That
alone makes the question of Lincoln's views on race an obviously significant one.

The truth is, if the Great Emancipator's early views on
"Negroes" were to be articulated by any American politician
today, that politician would be stamped a blatant racist and
condemned by most voters as unfit even for the lowest public office. A respected author and editor, Lerone Bennett, Jr.,
of *Ebony* magazine described Lincoln precisely that way a
few years ago in a book called *Forced into Slavery: Abraham Lincoln's White Dream.* The book was condemned by white Lincoln scholars from James McPherson to Eric Foner, with
one magazine critic calling it a "furious screed."[130] The author maintains that Lincoln supported noxious laws like the
Fugitive Slave Act and the Illinois black codes and anti-
immigration laws and regularly used demeaning descriptions
of blacks. Bennett contends that Lincoln perpetrated something of a fraud by his Emancipation Proclamation, advo-

---

130. Jack E. White, "Was Lincoln a Racist?" *Time*, May 15, 2000: 76.

cated compensated emigration of freed blacks to Africa, and otherwise entertained what Bennett called a dream of a "Lily White America." Bennett went so far as to state that, by issuing the Emancipation Proclamation, Lincoln "re-enslaved and/or condemned to extended slavery more blacks than he ever freed"; and that "if he had his way, millions of twentieth-century whites would have been in *Gone With the Wind* instead of watching it."[131] (It should be noted that Congressman Jesse Jackson, Jr., in his own book, *A More Perfect Union*, stated unhesitatingly, "Abraham Lincoln freed the slaves."[132])

Defenders of Lincoln argue that while Lincoln was not as enlightened on race as most modern politicians are, he did insist on limiting the spread of slavery in order to place it "in the course of ultimate extinction." He was also prepared to ennoble the fight to save the Union by using the war to end slavery everywhere, and he was willing to utter the first words any American president had ever spoken that advocated education and voting rights for freed people of color.

Mr. Bennett is black, but there are other distinguished white authors who attest to the accuracy of some of Bennett's descriptions, occasionally in equally forceful language. Garry Wills, for example, cited Lincoln's 1858 speech in Charleston, Illinois, as an example of his early racism. That day, in his third debate with the unabashedly racist Democratic senator Stephen A. Douglas, Lincoln felt it necessary

---

131. Lerone Bennett, *Forced into Glory: Abraham Lincoln's White Dream* (Chicago: Johnson Publishing, 2000), 13, 20.

132. Jesse L. Jackson, Jr., and Frank E. Watkins, *A More Perfect Union: Advancing New American Rights* (New York: Welcome Rain Publishers, 2001), 161.

to repudiate suggestions that he favored civil rights for blacks. He did so in language calculated to amuse his audience—modern readers can determine this from the on-the-scene stenographers' reports of the crowd's laughter and applause—but he did so in language that has, not unfairly, haunted him in history.[133]

> I will say then that I am not, nor ever have been in favor of bringing about in any way the social and political equality of the white and black races,—that I am not nor ever have been in favor of making voters or jurors of negroes, nor of qualifying them to hold office, nor to intermarry with white people; and I will say in addition to this that there is a physical difference between the white and black races which I believe will forever forbid the two races living together on terms of social and political equality.[134]

Wills goes on to point out what he calls other crude and demagogic references by Lincoln to "negroes" that were apparently designed to soften the political impact of his anti-slavery position with voters accustomed to judging blacks as inferior to whites and to deflect charges by Douglas that he was a closet abolitionist whose election would encourage blacks and whites to fraternize on terms of perfect equal-

133. Garry Wills, *Lincoln at Gettysburg* (New York: Simon & Schuster, 1995), 76–83.
134. *Collected Works*, 3:145–46. Lincoln did hasten to add: "I do not perceive that because the white man is to have the superior position the negro should be denied everything. I do not understand that because I do not want a negro woman for a slave I must necessarily want her for a wife. My understanding is that I can just let her alone."

ity—an untenable political position for any mainstream white politician in the racist America of the 1850s.

There are not many respected scholars or authors who would deny Lincoln held these unsavory racial views before he assumed the presidency. Indeed, David Herbert Donald urges us not even to try to palliate Lincoln's uglier statements by saying he grew up in a racist society or that his ideas were shared by many contemporaries—which they were—because, "After all there were numerous Americans of his generation—notably, many of them abolitionists—who were committed to racial equality."[135] Donald was speaking of a personal racial equality that went far beyond the right not to be enslaved.

Frederick Douglass was, of course, one such advocate. This great black intellectual and former slave, who eventually came to admire Lincoln and to credit him with the indispensable contribution he made to freeing blacks, pointed out that in his earlier years Lincoln was principally devoted to the welfare of whites—opposed to the spread of slavery but willing to accept it where it already existed. As Douglass saw it, while Lincoln "hated slavery, and really desired its destruction, he always proceeded against it in a manner the least likely to shock or drive from him any who were truly in sympathy with the preservation of the Union, but who were not friendly to emancipation."[136]

---

135. See for example: Donald, *Lincoln*, 721; Charles B. Strozier, *Lincoln on Democracy*, 103; Richard Nelson Current, *Speaking of Abraham Lincoln* (Urbana: University of Illinois Press, 1983), 32–33.

136. *Life and Times of Frederick Douglass Written by Himself* (1893), quoted in Henry Louis Gates, Jr., *Frederick Douglass* (New York: Library of America, 1994), 793.

Douglass's opinion of Lincoln changed with the benefit of passing years and personal acquaintance. As Lincoln progressed politically he grew in understanding and sensitivity. His brilliant leadership helped preserve the Union and was the indispensable moving force behind the constitutional amendments that won freedom for the slaves and lifted the Constitution closer to the aspirations set forth in the Declaration of Independence. Douglass acknowledged that Lincoln had more than redeemed himself for whatever unpleasant views he might have held about "negroes" in his earlier years.

On inauguration day, 1865, as Lincoln delivered his immortal "malice toward none" address and commenced his second term as president, Douglass looked on from the audience. He thought that Lincoln's declaration—that God might will the war to continue "until every drop of blood drawn with the lash, shall be paid by another drawn with the sword"—was nothing short of "wonderful" and "remarkable." Later that day, Douglass was reminded that the road to equality was still paved with humiliating obstacles. When he tried to enter the East Room to join the post-inauguration reception, he was barred by White House guards until Lincoln spotted him. Lincoln's "countenance lighted up," and he ushered him in, gave him a "cordial" handshake, and asked him his opinion of his speech, declaring, "There is no man's opinion that I value more than yours." Douglass reckoned that it was not only the first time in his own life that he had attended a White House event but also "the first time in any colored man's life." A painful reminder of the attitudes of the times is that this great man came close to being shown out of the White House through a plank leading to a window![137]

In 1876 Douglass expressed his belief that Lincoln "was preeminently the white man's president, entirely devoted to the welfare of white men," and that blacks "were not the special objects of his consideration . . . We were at best his stepchildren; children by adoption, children by forces of circumstances and necessity." But while Douglass believed that "viewed from the genuine abolition ground, Mr. Lincoln seemed tardy, cold, dull, and indifferent," he acknowledged that "measuring him by the sentiment of his country, he was swift, zealous, radical, and determined."[138]

In his final assessment of the late president written nine years after those comments and twenty years after Lincoln's death, Douglass recalled, "In all my interviews with Mr. Lincoln I was impressed with his entire freedom from popular prejudice against the colored race. He was the first great man that I talked with in the United States freely, who in no single instance reminded me of the difference between himself and myself, of the difference of color, and I thought that all the more remarkable because he came from a State where there were black laws.[139]

137. Frederick Douglass in Allen Thorndike Rice, ed., *Reminiscences of Lincoln by Distinguished Men of His Time* (New York: North American Publishing, 1886), 191–92. Douglass actually paraphrased the excerpt imperfectly; this text quotes the original, from *Collected Works*, 8:333.

138. Philip S. Foner, ed., *Frederick Douglass: Selected Speeches and Writings* (abridged ed., Chicago: Lawrence Hill Books, 1999), 618–19, 621. Douglass delivered these remarks at the dedication of the unveiling of the Freedmen's Monument to Lincoln in Washington on April 14, 1876.

139. Rice, *Reminiscences of Abraham Lincoln*, 193.

A generation later, Douglass's widely acknowledged successor as the leader of the black community, Booker T. Washington, marked the centennial of Lincoln's birth by predicting that his "spirit of freedom and fair play will never cease to spread and grow in power till throughout the world all men shall know the truth, and the truth shall make them free." Lincoln, he believed, "was in the truest sense great because he unfettered himself . . . climbed out of the valley, where his vision was narrowed and weakened by the fog and miasma, onto the mountain top, where in a pure and unclouded atmosphere he could see the truth which enabled him to rate all men at their true worth."[140]

Douglass and Washington might well be surprised by some of the charges being leveled against Lincoln today that suggest the president did not change his views as he matured and faced the prospect of a biracial society in an America free of slavery.

More significant today than the rather one-sided historical debate about Lincoln's early racial views is the sad reality that for all the glory of Lincoln's Civil War triumph, the work he set out to do remains tragically unfinished, particularly concerning the rights of African Americans and other minorities.

Abraham Lincoln attempted to lift enslaved blacks to their feet, freeing them from slavery and empowering them as American citizens equal to all others in rights. But for one

---

140. Booker T. Washington, "My Tribute to the Great Emancipator," New York City, February 12, 1909, in Waldo C. Braden, ed., *Building the Myth: Selected Speeches Memorializing Abraham Lincoln* (Urbana: University of Illinois Press, 1990), 154.

hundred years thereafter, our laws and many white Americans continued bitter and hurtful discrimination against African Americans. Then came 1929: the year that brought us the Great Depression also brought us the birth of Michael Luther King, later renamed Martin, who lifted the wagon where it had been left by Lincoln and pulled it farther up the mountain. As a pastor in Alabama nearly a hundred years after the Thirteenth Amendment, King launched a struggle to redeem the promise of the Declaration of Independence—and of Lincoln's "second Declaration of Independence," the Emancipation Proclamation. Nearly a century later, despite all of Lincoln's heroic work, many blacks of the 1950s were still prohibited from voting, attending public schools or colleges, serving on juries, living in certain neighborhoods, sharing public facilities as equals, or getting work in white-owned businesses.

In some parts of the country blacks were not even allowed to keep a seat on a bus if a white person wanted it or to walk on the same sidewalk with whites who didn't want to share it with them. With his only weapons being an extraordinary intelligence, a unique oratorical ability, passionate commitment, and a belief in nonviolent civil disobedience, King became one of the great leaders in American history and produced a campaign that led to the passage of the Civil Rights Act of 1964. The WHITES ONLY signs came down. The law ordered voting booths, public places, and business opportunities to be opened and available to blacks and others alike. The public schools that had technically been desegregated by the Supreme Court's decision in *Brown v. Board of Education* in 1954 became more open than they had been.

Sadly, however, it still left us a long way from the fulfillment of Lincoln's dream and the reasonable expectations open-minded Americans might still have.

At the 1963 March on Washington, King reminded America of "the fierce urgency of *now*," as he stood at a "hallowed spot"—the Lincoln Memorial—to remind the country that the "great beacon of light" extended by that "great American" had burned too briefly. Emancipation—the "joyous daybreak" that ended "a long night of captivity"—had failed to generate the uninterrupted progress that Lincoln dreamed of. Now King dreamed aloud for his own generation. It proved a transcendent moment that inflected both urgency and prophecy into Lincoln's unfinished work. "*Now*," King reiterated, "is the time to make real the promises of democracy . . . to lift our nation from the quicksands of racial injustice to the solid rock of brotherhood."[141]

In many ways, we have not quite yet advanced from quicksand to bedrock. That is not to disparage all that is good about our unique United States of America. We are still the greatest nation in the world and the most effective engine of opportunity in the world. But great as this nation is, we have not yet corrected the damage created by the years of horrendous slavery that produced riches and comfort for the whites by demeaning, debasing, and debilitating blacks.

The stubbornly lingering evidence of failure is apparent everywhere around us. Schools in predominantly black areas are still not as good as schools in white areas. Discrimination

---

141. Martin Luther King, Jr., address at the March on Washington, August 28, 1963, in Caroline Kennedy, ed., *A Patriot's Handbook* (New York: Hyperion, 2000), 321–22.

against blacks in the business world and beyond still exists. As a result, blacks today are more apt to be inadequately educated, unemployed, poor, uninsured, ill, imprisoned, or sentenced to death, than whites are. Blacks earn less; they are much less likely to be wealthy CEOs or important public officials.

We have never had a black president or vice president; the occasional national candidacies, by Jesse Jackson, Shirley Chisholm, Alan Keyes, Rev. Al Sharpton, and Carol Mosley Braun, have been quietly or noisily dismissed by pundits as more symbolic than serious. We don't have a single black in the ranks of the dominant majority party in the House— the party of Lincoln, no less—nor a single black senator. More than a century after Hiram Revels of Alabama briefly took Jefferson Davis's old seat in the Senate—becoming the first black to serve in that body—Massachusetts Senator Edward Brooke is merely a memory, and Illinois's Mosley Braun has departed Washington after a single term during which, arguably, she was held to a far higher standard by the press and electorate than has ever been applied to her white colleagues—including, infamously, the longest-serving senator of them all, Strom Thurmond, who not only perpetuated segregation and racism but secretly fathered a child with an African American servant in the manner of the plantation masters of old.

Today even modest efforts to compensate for the debility created by the historic injustice of slavery and discrimination are difficult to sustain. Schools are being resegregated. This, the richest nation in the world, continues to allow 35 million Americans—one in five of all children and one in two black children—to live in poverty, 44 million Americans to go without health insurance, the public schools to deteriorate, and some 9 million Americans to remain unemployed.

We have come a long way in 229 years, but we have left many Americans behind—a disproportionate number of them black. Lincoln tried to teach us how much better off we would be if we had fewer poor and deprived Americans and more well-educated Americans prepared to be productive and useful. If instead of tying one arm behind our backs as we have for so long, we were able to build and grow, using both hands, with everyone participating equally, *all* our African Americans, *all* our Hispanics, all our Asians, *all* our women—all our *Americans—equally!*, the United States would be as our forefathers promised in the Declaration of Independence; as the Thirteenth Amendment suggests; and as the Civil Rights Act insists; as justice, decency, and intelligence require; and as Abraham Lincoln struggled so heroically to assure.

From the moment African Americans took up arms to fight for their own freedom—to make a practical reality of the promise of the Emancipation Proclamation—Lincoln recognized the nation's historic debt to Americans who had been brought here against their will, forced to labor without compensation, condemned to noncitizenship by our courts, and forced even when liberated to live as perpetual inferiors in a society nominally dedicated to equality.

Addressing the citizens of his old Springfield, Illinois, hometown—where as a young man he had acquired the kind of racism he shed as president—Lincoln made abundantly clear that these inequities had to be corrected. In a letter to James C. Conkling that he meant to be read aloud at a pro-union rally, Lincoln warned whites to understand this about the black veterans of the struggle for Union and freedom:

> [T]here will be some black men who can remember that, with silent tongue, and clenched teeth, and steady eye, and well-poised bayonet, they have helped mankind on to this great consummation; while, I fear, there will be some white ones, unable to forget that, with malignant heart, and deceitful speech, they have strove to hinder it.[142]

"Thus," Lincoln insisted later that year, "we have the new reckoning." Our failure, thus far, to achieve that reckoning in full must stand as the single, most lamentable unfinished work of Lincoln's timeless promise to his country.[143]

---

142. *Collected Works*, 6:410.

143. From the third annual message to Congress, December 8, 1863, in ibid., 7:50.

"ABRAHAM LINCOLN'S" 2004
ADDRESS TO CONGRESS

UNLIKE HIS best-known, best-loved speeches, Abraham
Lincoln's four annual messages to Congress were more
prose than poetry. That is because their principal purpose
was to report the work of government and gently suggest
the problems he believed needed to be addressed in the
year ahead. Lincoln did not deliver these precursors to
today's State of the Union addresses in person; he simply
submitted them to Congress in writing where they were
read to a joint session by a clerk. With this in mind and in
an attempt to adapt Lincoln's tone—no one can ever fully
replicate his style—what follows is an approximation of
what his message might have sounded like had he been
president in January of 2004, with the positions on current
issues formulated from the discussion set out in this book.
Some phrases written by Lincoln nearly a century and a
half ago have been inculcated into this text and resonate
with striking applicability: they have been identified here
along with their sources.

Annual Message to Congress 2004

FELLOW-CITIZENS of the Senate and House of Representatives.[144]

In the midst of unprecedented troubles, extraordinary threats to our safety from foreign enemies, apparently not acting on behalf of any particular nation or nations of the world but rather for their own evil purposes, through acts of violence and threats of such acts, we nevertheless have cause to express great gratitude to God for our continuing favorable condition as a nation. The national resources remain unexhausted and, as we believe, unexhaustible.[145]

It remains true that people of many nations around the world are eager to come to our land to avail themselves of the freedom and opportunity that have sustained, and permitted to thrive, many millions of immigrants for more than two hundred years. They constitute one of the principal replenishing streams that are appointed by Providence to repair the ravages of war and its wastes of national strength and wealth. With thanks to these courageous and enterprising legions of seekers and strugglers, and the beneficent God that has chosen to smile upon us, we humbly acknowledge that we have built the largest economy and most powerful military in the world, and an engine of opportunity

---

144. Lincoln used this precise salutation in his first, and all subsequent, messages to Congress. See, as the first example, his 1861 message in *Collected Works*, 5:35.

145. "unprecedented troubles," ibid.; "great . . . God," in ibid.; "The national . . . unexhaustible," from the 1864 annual message to Congress, in ibid., 8:151.

so prolifically successful as to be the wonder and admiration of the whole world.[146]

Surrounded by these undeniable proofs of our unique accomplishments, we might be tempted now to aspire to *no* new heights, enjoying our gifts and achievements, pressing ourselves only enough to deal with searching out and disabling our future enemies, who without intervention might perpetuate their violence around the world and their threats to repeat their assaults upon our nation. The condition of our relations with other nations is less gratifying than it has usually been at former periods.[147] That must be corrected. To end the evils, great and small, which spring from want of sympathy from former foreign allies and enmity from others, whether nations or individuals, is one of the most important functions of our foreign policy.[148]

At the same time, we must not ignore the many urgent calls for relief and assistance from the larger part of our people who still have not benefited as they might, and as they should, from our tremendous abundance. From the beginning, we proposed to give *all* a chance; and we sought to help the weak to grow stronger, the ignorant, wiser; and all the better and happier together.[149]

---

146. "One of the . . . national strength and wealth," in *Collected Works*, 8:151; "wonder . . . world," from a speech at Kalamazoo, August 26, 1856, in ibid., 2:364.

147. "The condition . . . former periods," from the annual message to Congress, December 1, 1862, in ibid., 5:518.

148. "To end the evils . . . functions of," from an address before the Wisconsin State Agricultural Society, Milwaukee, September 30, 1859, in ibid., 3:471–72.

149. "we proposed . . . happier together," from a fragment on slavery, ca. July 1, 1854, in ibid., 2:222.

Among our 280 million people, only two in one hundred of the taxpayers are so wealthy that they have no great need that they cannot meet with their own means. By far, the overwhelming majority of us continue to struggle either not to slide down the economic ladder of the nation or merely to begin climbing it. No doubt many of those that I—and, I trust, most of you—would describe as struggling or impoverished, would in many other much poorer nations than ours be regarded as sustaining themselves and their families admirably. But for us to accept that lower standard—while allowing the great economic disparities in our own country to grow, notwithstanding the abundance of resources, that, if properly employed, could make life safer and more productive for all of us—would be a travesty of justice, a denial of our fundamental principles as a nation, and an act of ingratitude to the Providence that has provided us with those resources. A decent respect for our citizens requires us to use our resources in ways that would benefit those of our people who, although deserving, have not enjoyed as much progress as those more fortunate. Whatever is calculated to advance the condition of the honest, struggling, laboring man, so far as my judgment will enable me to judge of a correct thing, I am for that thing.[150]

But more than that, to the extent that we deem ourselves comfortable here at home, should we not consider devoting a larger portion of our abundance than we have so far to those desperately needy in foreign lands living on the same globe

---

150. "Whatever is calculated . . . I am for that thing," from a speech to Germans in Cincinnati, February 12, 1861, in *Collected Works*, 4:203.

we all occupy as the great family of men?[151] Especially those
with whom we seek to improve our current relationships.

With those assumptions I call upon you, who make the
laws, to adopt the following measures as soon as possible
and convenient to your own circumstances.

Instead of pressing forward with all of the tax reduc-
tions you have adopted in recent years in considerable part
on the mistaken assumption that we did not need those resources because we would enjoy a tremendous surplus in our
federal budget, which in fact is now laden with a great deficit
instead, I ask you to make changes to correct some of what
has been done. I make the request because I go for all sharing the privileges of the government who assist in bearing its
burdens, and because the benefits must extend not just to
the wealthy few but the many poor:[152]

- Defer that portion of the tax cuts payable over the
  next several years, in value more than one trillion dollars, that would have gone to the wealthiest 1 percent of
  the taxpayers, until we have returned to the budget surplus you had assumed in giving the tax cuts in the first
  place.

---

151. "great family of men," in *Collected Works,* 4:203.
152. "I go for all sharing . . . bearing its burdens," from a letter to the *Sangamo Journal,*
June 13, 1836, in ibid., 1:48; "wealthy few" and "many poor" from a letter to
William S. Wait, March 2, 1839, in ibid., 149. In the same letter, Lincoln pointed
out on the subject of tax policy: "The wealthy can not *justly* complain, because
the change is equitable within itself, and also a *sine qua non* to a compliance with
the Constitution. If, however, the wealthy should, regardless of the justness of the
complaint, as men often are, when interest is involved in the question, complain
of the change, it is still to be remembered, that *they* are not sufficiently numerous
to carry the elections."

- Allocate the one trillion dollars in four parts, which together would increase the productivity of our workers,
advance the comfort of and assist in meeting the needs
of our unfortunately unemployed or disabled, strengthen
our economy, and reduce the grotesque debt that we
have already incurred on ourselves and that we are plac-
ing like a great albatross around the neck of future generations of Americans, ignoring the impropriety of
borrowing money to pay interest on borrowed money.[153]

The four parts are as follows, and I leave it to you to
suggest the specific portions for each:

1. Deficit reduction. A new national debt, has been created,
   and is still growing on us with a rapidity fearful to
   contemplate.[154]
2. Enhancement of education (the most important subject
   which we as a people can be engaged in), job training,
   and health care, to provide workers with the skills
   needed to compete in an increasingly competitive world
   economy, and to protect those who have not been able
   to procure health insurance.[155]
3. Increased tax cuts for workers in the lower economic
   brackets and assistance to the 15 million or so workers
   who are officially designated unemployed, are actually

153. "impropriety ... borrowed money," from a speech to the Illinois State Legislature, December 4, 1840, in *Collected Works*, 1:216.
154. "A new ... contemplate," from a Whig Party campaign circular, March 4,
1843, in ibid., 1:311.
155. "the most ... engaged in," from a message to voters in Sangamon County,
March 9, 1832, in ibid., 1:8.

unemployed but no longer seeking employment because of the futility of their search, or are only working part-time and not able to meet their needs.

4. Assistance to our states and local governments in order to avoid regressive tax increases at those levels; to enhance the security of our homeland; to avoid the firing of teachers, health-care workers, police officers, and first responders in emergencies; and to repair some of the nation's badly deteriorated infrastructure, for internal improvements of this broad and goodly land are a mighty interest.[156]

It seems to me that these suggestions present no serious challenge to any fundamental political beliefs held by any of the distinguished members of this Congress, whatever particular symbol—elephant, donkey, or neither—that you may wear upon your lapel. Rather, I believe they are supported or even demanded by the most significant of the fundamental principles that define this great nation and that have promoted our progress. Together, our basic law—the Constitution animated and uplifted by the spirit of the Declaration of Independence that immortal emblem of humanity—has created the most effective political instrument in world history, as demonstrated by the record of the last two hundred years.[157] It did so by providing us with a well-ordered liberty and a coalescence of our powerful instinct

---

156. "internal improvements . . . mighty interest," from speech to Congress on internal improvements, June 22, 1848, in *Collected Works*, 1:488.

157. "that . . . humanity," from speech in Lewiston, Illinois, August 17, 1858, in ibid., 2:547.

for individual ambition, effort, and accountability together with the indispensable need for a dynamic sense of community that recognizes our interconnectedness and interdependence and valued cooperation over conflict. We can succeed only by concert.[158] Our defense is in the preservation of the spirit which prizes liberty as the heritage of all men, in all lands, everywhere. Destroy this spirit, and you have planted the seeds of despotism around your own doors.[159]

That capacity to share benefits and burdens as a united society, for the good of all, has grown over the years as the distances between and among us have shrunk by the grace of the evolving technologies of transportation and communication. Today that capacity is more important to our nation, and to this world, than it has ever been—and no political theory worthy of mention can refute that obvious reality. We will be regularly reminded of that on September 11 for all the scores of years to come.

On 9/11 of 2004, we will once again pause to remember heroes and heroines—the honored dead—of that singular day of horror three years earlier and to recall the terrible toll in human lives that began the war against terrorism that continues to preoccupy us.[160]

Now we must defend ourselves by thwarting terrorists, those who aid them, and those who shelter them.

---

158. "We can succeed only by concert," from the annual message to Congress, December 1, 1862, in *Collected Works*, 5:537.

159. "Our defense . . . your own doors," from a speech in Edwardsville, Illinois, September 11, 1858, in ibid., 3:95.

160. "honored dead," from the Gettysburg Address, November 19, 1863, in ibid., 7:18.

It is a war being fought not over the possession of land but over ideas. We are not opposed by great armies of hostile nations but by irrationally enraged people, many of whom believe themselves to be messengers of a religious faith that demands the destruction of our supposedly infidel nation. This belief is a distortion of their Muslim religion. In fact, we both pray to the same God; and, properly understood, that God and the better angels of our nature require that we be not enemies but friends.[161] The terrorists have been misled into believing otherwise. They rouse themselves to anger and ferocity by retelling the history of the Crusades when misguided and evil hordes of western Christians savagely murdered their Muslim forebearers. The attempts by today's Christians to convince the world that they have been long separated from that abominable aberration is largely unavailing. Indeed, these Muslims contend that we in this nation, and some other Westerners, continue our unfair treatment of them by aiding their oppressors in the Middle East and particularly in what is today Israel. They also argue that we have failed to share the great material benefits that our good fortune and hard work have produced with the millions of their own people who have remained impoverished and despairing.

Their tactics consist of an incessant series of stealthy attacks, often by zealous suicide bombers, against targets of opportunity around the world—always identifiable as friends of the "Great Satan," the name they apply to us,

---

161. "pray to the same God," in *Collected Works*, 8:333; "the better angels of our nature," from the first inaugural address, March 4, 1861, ibid., 4:271.

that sums up so graphically their hatred of the United States.

They are apparently led by Osama bin Laden and al-Qaeda. These leaders are sworn killers, lethal tumors that must be extirpated from the family of man. We have no choice but to fight them when they attack, to search them out when they hide, and to treat as enemies those who assist or encourage them. At the same time, however, we must do all we can to use only the force that is clearly necessary, avoiding as far as it is possible taking innocent lives or violating our own Constitution. There is no glory in taking life—and often great shame. War, at the best, is terrible. This war has deranged business, it has destroyed property and ruined homes around the globe. In our country, it has helped produce a huge national debt.[162]

So, too, we have learned from our experiences in the past that the urgency of war can tempt our leaders to avoid, distort or unnecessarily surrender constitutional principles of freedom and privacy, which are our greatest strength. I have myself been accused of doing so in another and earlier emergency. I made my explanation then and will not repeat it today especially since I suspect most of you are already familiar with it. Allow me only to say that whatever the verdict of history concerning my conduct then, it is clear our current engagement with terrorism, which will in all likelihood continue into the indefinite future, does not, for all its seriousness, present a danger to our country's existence equal to

---

162. "War . . . this country," from a speech at the Philadelphia Sanitary Fair, June 16, 1864, in *Collected Works*, 7:394.

that which prompted my reluctant but limited suspension of liberties in the past.

What constitutes the bulwark of our own liberty and independence? It is not our frowning battlements, our bristling sea coasts, our missiles, or the strength of our gallant and disciplined armed forces. These are not our most important safeguard against the terrorizing of our fair land: Our principal reliance must be on the *love of liberty* which God has planted in our bosoms.[163]

Therefore, my disputed actions in the past are a precedent that may be safely ignored today. Either they will be considered wrong and should be ignored for that reason, or they will be considered right but for reasons that do not pertain in the current emergency.

With that prudent caution we will continue our struggle against terrorists whenever and wherever we confront them. At the same time, we know that destroying terrorists, driven by their mad delusion and hating us so much that they are eager to surrender their own lives in order to take ours, will not end terrorism. Indeed, destroying terrorists tends to inspire more terrorism, as it has so evidently and tragically in Israel and Palestine. In addition to removing the tumors, we must deal with the disease that produces terrorists—the hate caused by a misunderstanding of what we are and what we intend. That will require that we find ways—no matter how difficult a task it is to end the hostilities in Israel and Palestine—to correct the distorted and provocative lessons being taught to Muslims and to move swiftly in Afghanistan,

---

163. "What constitutes . . . our bosoms," from speech at Edwardsville, Illinois, September 11, 1858, in *Collected Works,* 3:95.

Iraq, and other Arab lands to introduce the kind of democratic government that will end oppression by replacing it with opportunities like those we so cherish in our own land.

Had I been president a year ago, I would not have invaded the nation of Iraq when we did. I would have tried harder to extend the process of looking for weapons of mass destruction, which, as it now appears, probably would have turned up nothing worthy of a war at that time. We were then in the midst of even more urgent business than removing the tyrant Saddam Hussein from power. We were in pursuit of Osama bin Laden and al-Qaeda who were responsible for 9/11 and who today continue to lead the terrorist efforts against us. I believe it was a mistake to divert our energies, our attention, and our forces to Iraq and away from the clearer, greater, more urgent terrorist threat. But we must not dwell in the past. What needs to be done lies ahead. With that in mind, I wish you to know that I am planning an extended international journey to Europe, the Middle East, Japan, and Russia in an attempt to rekindle the flame of brotherhood and unity that bound us together in the past with our major allies and to light such a fire where there was not one before.

I do so in recognition of the fact that as mighty as we are, we need the rest of the world as much as the rest of the world needs us if we are to do what must be done to create a more perfect union at home and a more perfect world beyond our shores. We will use force when it is regrettably but clearly required and only then. Whenever we can find the opportunity we will try by our actions to convince our enemies—and our friends—that the Creator who made us equal to one another and blessed us with the inalienable rights of life, liberty, and the pursuit of happiness is their Creator as well.

As I said on the day I took the oath of presidential office for the second time, so I say now: With malice toward none, with charity for all, with firmness in the right as God gives us to see the right, let us strive on to finish the work we are in; to do all which may achieve a just and a lasting peace among ourselves and with all nations.[164]

We of this Congress and this administration, will be remembered in spite of ourselves. No personal significance, or insignificance, can spare one or another of us. The trial through which we pass, will light us down, in honor or dishonor, to the latest generation. The way is plain, peaceful, generous, just—a way which, if followed, the world will forever applaud, and God must forever bless.[165]

Thanks to all. For the great republic—for the principle it lives by, and keeps alive—for man's vast future—thanks to all.[166]

164. "With malice . . . all nations," second inaugural address, March 4, 1865, in *Collected Works*, 8:333.

165. "We of this Congress . . . God must forever bless," from the message to Congress, December 1, 1862, in ibid., 5:537.

166. "Thanks to all . . . thanks to all," from a letter read aloud to the citizens of Springfield, Illinois, August 26, 1863, in ibid., 6:410.

ACKNOWLEDGMENTS

THIS BOOK GREW out of a lifelong interest in Abraham Lincoln and a growing concern that America's leaders are in danger of ignoring Lincoln's invaluable and timeless lessons about government, opportunity, equality, and this nation's role as an object lesson for the world.

Nearly fifty years ago my sister, Marie, gave me as a gift Roy P. Basler's celebrated nine-volume *Collected Works of Abraham Lincoln.* I have been reading Lincoln ever since and from the very beginning, I found myself gripped by the beauty of his prose and the searing impact of his logic. In later years when I became involved in public service, I used Lincoln as a yardstick to help measure our commitment to his dreams of self-determination, freedom, and the making of a more perfect union.

In 1989 I was reminded again, more powerfully than ever before, of Lincoln's reputation as the representative American, and of America's responsibility to live up to his example. That summer a delegation of teachers from the Polish Solidarity Movement visited the State Capitol in Albany. It was during my seventh year as governor of New York and I had been asked to extend the greetings of our people. As these heroic teachers were taking their leave, one of them asked me what works on the subject of democracy I might recommend to restock bookshelves that had been all but emptied under two generations of totalitarian censorship. My answer was: "Lincoln." Lincoln, they responded, was not available to them; he had long ago been erased from the curriculum in Poland, banned by Communist rulers' suspicions about his beliefs in equal opportunity and human rights. I promised to do what I could to restore Lincoln to his proper place with the Polish people and called on my friend and colleague, Harold Holzer, to work with me to produce a new Lincoln collection. The result, created with a cadre of historian-advisers and contributors, was the 1990 book *Lincoln on Democracy*, a compendium of Lincoln's timeless words on liberty and equality, which was not only issued in Polish and presented in bulk to Solidarity leader Lech Walesa himself but was also eventually published in English, Japanese, Hebrew, and even Indonesian.

This was one of the most rewarding and, I think, useful projects of my time in office—and my only regret is that a plan to publish an edition in Arabic fell victim to the growing tensions in the Middle East. I believed then, and believe now, that Lincoln's pure love of freedom can do more to keep nations in harmony than any words ever written by an elected official anytime, anywhere.

Ever since the *Lincoln on Democracy* project, I hoped to find an opportunity to look again into the Lincoln theme and find a way not only to advance and reconsider his rich and beautiful prose but also to interpret and apply his wisdom for the modern world. The opportunity dramatically presented itself just before the ceremony commemorating the first anniversary of 9/11 when the governor of New York state, George Pataki; the mayor of New York, Michael Bloomberg; and the former mayor Rudy Giuliani, all announced that instead of offering their own thoughts and words at the ceremony they would read the words of Abraham Lincoln. That inspired an obvious question: If Lincoln can be helpful in providing insight and comfort concerning one of the most significant events in our nation's history that occurred 136 years after his death, why not consult him concerning other serious challenges we face? This book attempts to do just that.

"Writing," Lincoln once said, "is the great invention of the world." I am grateful that he left his own great writings to us and am proud to have been given the opportunity to examine them again and seek from them instruction about how to deal with today's challenges. My hope is that this book brings Lincoln back into the current conversation of American politics where he so firmly belongs.

I am grateful to my wife, Matilda, for her patience and support in this endeavor as with everything I have done and tried to do for the years since our marriage in 1954 and to my children and grandchildren for forgiving my numerous preoccupations.

I am also grateful to a number of others who helped produce this book, particularly Jane Isay, our bright, ingenious, and courageous editor at Harcourt, Inc., whose confidence in the effort never wavered, even when our own enthusiasm exceeded our productivity; David Hough, the managing editor at Harcourt whose final editing improved the language and clarified my intended meaning immeasurably; Mary Porcelli, my secretary, who added long hours of transcribing to her already heavy, normal workload; and my sister, Marie, for her gift of the *Collected Works* without which I may never have been properly introduced to the wonderful world of Lincoln. Thanks as well to Chief Justice Frank Williams whose vigorous reading and insightful suggestions helped me avoid misinterpretations and preserve accuracy, and Bill O'Shaughnessy, Rock Brynner, Floss Frucher, Jack Newfield, and Fabian Palomino, whose constructive criticism—although occasionally painful—improved the book.

Perhaps one group involved with Lincoln more than any other deserves the gratitude of all of us in this country: the many historians, scholars, and authors who have devoted themselves to the preservation, interpretation, and dissemination of Lincoln's words and wisdom for nearly 150 years. Among them I owe a particular debt to the distinguished scholars and authors who contributed to *Lincoln on Democracy* in 1990: Gabor S. Boritt, Richard Nelson Current, William E. Gienapp, James M. McPherson, Mark E. Neely, Jr., Charles B. Strozier, Hans L. Trefousse, in addition to Chief Justice Williams.

Most of all, I thank Harold Holzer, whom I have known for half of his life and who has been an important part of mine since 1977. He was a crucial contributor to this book in his role as historical adviser and as a coauthor of the section in this book titled "Lincoln as Political Scripture." Few scholars know more about Lincoln, and even fewer understand how crucial it is not to relegate Lincoln to the past but to use him for the future. The simple truth is that

this book could not have been produced without his knowl-
edge, advice, consultation, and validation. On the other
hand, whatever deficiencies it may have are unquestionably
attributable to my unassisted efforts.

—MARIO M. CUOMO

NEW YORK

FEBRUARY 12, 2004